W9-CRJ-326

A Time For Freedom

A Time For Freedom

What Happened When in America

SIMON & SCHUSTER
New York • London • Toronto • Sydney

SIMON & SCHUSTER
1230 Avenue of the Americas, New York, New York 10020

Book design by Dan Potash
The text for this book is set in Celestia Antique.
Manufactured in the United States of America
2 4 6 8 10 9 7 5 3
Library of Congress Cataloging-in-Publication Data
Cheney, Lynne V.
A time for freedom : what happened when in America / Lynne Cheney.
— 1st ed.
p. cm.
ISBN-13: 978-1-4169-0925-5
ISBN-10: 1-4169-0925-7
1. United States—History—Chronology. I. Title.
E174.5.C525 2005
973'.02'02—dc22
2005019136

Editor's Note: Archaic spelling and capitalization in historical quotations have been modernized throughout the text.

To my daughters, Liz and Mary

ACKNOWLEDGMENTS

My first thanks are to my talented research assistant at the American Enterprise Institute, Elisabeth Irwin, who put enormous time and effort into *A Time for Freedom* while at the same time skillfully managing many other projects underway. I would also like to thank John Fonte and Wilfred McClay for their ongoing advice and insights about matters historical. This book benefited immensely from their involvement.

Many of my colleagues at the American Enterprise Institute have provided valuable guidance, including AEI president Christopher DeMuth, resident fellow Karlyn Bowman, and Director of Economic Policy Studies Kevin Hassett. Kate Campaigne, Gordon Gray, and Kathryn Newmark of the AEI staff were of assistance, as were interns Amy Bastian and Lisa Valentine. I thank all of them, as I do researcher Kate Rick.

I've been extremely fortunate to work with an amazing team at Simon & Schuster, starting at the top with CEO Jack Romanos and president of Children's Publishing, Rick Richter. My thoughtful editor, Paula Wiseman, provided many valuable suggestions, and I am grateful as well for her enthusiastic support of this project. My gratitude also to creative director Dan Potash, Jessica Sonkin, and Steve Kennedy and to Lee Wade, Lisa Ford, Chava Wolin, Dorothy Gribbin, Erica Stahler, Toby Greenberg, Hilary Goodman, Alexandra Penfold, and Caroline Abbey. In addition, I would like to acknowledge the contributions of Suzanne Murphy, Tracy van Straaten, Jennifer Zatorski, and Michelle Montague.

Attorney Bob Barnett has once again been my wise and cheerful guide to the world of publishing, and once again I thank him very much.

CONTENTS

INTRODUCTION

No one can fully appreciate the great good fortune we have to be Americans without knowing the events that brought us to where we are today. Our freedom and strength are products of the past, and although the choices made by the brave men and women who preceded us do not offer sure guidance to the future, they offer the best guidance that we have.

Unfortunately, fewer and fewer of us are leaving school knowing the basic facts of our history. One study found that two thirds of seventeen-year-olds could not identify the half century in which the Civil War occurred. A survey of seniors at elite colleges and universities showed that only one out of five was familiar with the words of the Gettysburg Address. A significant number of seniors thought that Ulysses S. Grant was a general in the Revolutionary War.

Facts alone are not enough for understanding history, of course, but without the facts understanding is impossible. A full appreciation of the achievement represented by the Nineteenth Amendment, ratified in 1920, requires knowing that women first organized to work for the right to vote in 1848, more than seventy years before. Comprehending why the Civil War occurred in the 1860s requires knowing that our nation expanded dramatically in the 1840s. It was the question of whether new states would be free or slave that finally made it impossible to paper over the great moral contradiction that slavery represented in a nation dedicated to freedom.

Some dates ought to be locked in memory. I think of 1492, 1607, 1620, 1776, and 1787, for starters. But it is equally important to be familiar enough with the order of events so that one has a sense of

the progression of our national story. We should all understand that when the delegates to the Continental Congress declared that "all men are created equal," they provided more than a rationale for independence; they gave inspiration to generations of men and women whose struggles would make that ideal a reality for more and ever more Americans.

There have been missteps in our history and many a backward step, as this time line makes clear. But it also shows that the overall thrust of our story has been the expansion of human freedom. It took us a bloody war to get rid of slavery, but we did it. It took us too long to ensure voting rights for African Americans and to enfranchise women, but we did those things too. And if we have not always understood that our freedom is caught up with the freedom of people around the globe, we do now, and we fight for them as well as for ourselves.

I offer this time line as a way of encouraging study of the past, and I also hope it will spark conversation about what is truly important for us to know. I like to imagine that one of these days I will go into a classroom to talk about history, and an artist in the class will want to know why I left out Mary Cassatt, or a student interested in technology will declare that I didn't pay enough attention to railroads. And I will say that I chose to concentrate on political history in this time line, but there is so much more and it should be explored. Indeed, the history of the entire world ought to be a subject of interest for students, but in A *Time for Freedom* I have started with America. This is our home—and how lucky we are that it is.

Lynne Cheney

ONE

BEGINNINGS

More than 13,000 years ago

Early migrants to America arrive from Asia, perhaps across the Bering Land Bridge or possibly even by boat. Over thousands of years they will be followed by others, who will travel across North, Central, and South America.

More than 2,500 years ago

The Adena people begin building ceremonial earth mounds in what is today the midwestern and southeastern United States. Subsequent Indian cultures—the Hopewell and the Mississippian—will also build mounds, some very large.

THE LARGEST OF THE MOUNDS, PRESERVED ON THE SITE OF AN ANCIENT CITY CALLED CAHOKIA (NOW CAHOKIA MOUNDS STATE HISTORIC SITE IN ILLINOIS), ONCE HAD A MASSIVE BUILDING ATOP IT, PROBABLY A PALACE FOR THE PRINCIPAL RULER. A THOUSAND YEARS OLD, A HUNDRED FEET HIGH, AND BUILT ENTIRELY OF EARTH, THIS MOUND, CALLED MONKS MOUND, COVERS MORE THAN FOURTEEN ACRES.

More than 700 years ago

Anasazi Indians build cliff dwellings in the Mesa Verde region, in what is today southwestern Colorado.

Mesa Verde cliff dwelling ruins

500 years ago

Distinctive Indian cultures exist all across the area we now know as the United States. In the Northeast five Indian nations form the Iroquois Confederacy.

The number of Indians living in North America as the European age of exploration began is a matter of debate. According to a survey published in 1992, estimates in history textbooks range from two million to ten million.

1492

Under the sponsorship of King Ferdinand and Queen Isabella of Spain, Christopher Columbus and his crew sail three ships, the *Niña*, the *Pinta*, and the *Santa María*, more than three thousand nautical miles across the Atlantic. Hoping to find the Indies, Columbus lands instead on an island in the Bahamas that he names San Salvador, or "Holy Savior."

"Tierra! Tierra!"

—Rodrigo de Triana, lookout aboard Columbus's ship the *Pinta,* upon seeing land

The *Niña, Pinta,* and *Santa María*

Columbus made four voyages to the New World, which he persisted in believing was the Indies. He died ignorant of his real accomplishment.

"An age will come after many years when the ocean will loose the chains of things, and a huge land lie revealed."

—a prophecy in Seneca's *Medea*, a play Columbus knew well

"This prophecy was fulfilled by my father the admiral, in the year 1492."

—Ferdinand Columbus, writing alongside the prophecy in his father's copy of *Seneca*

1497

John Cabot, sailing for Henry VII of England, reaches North America aboard a small ship, the *Mathew*. Almost a century will pass, but his voyage will become the basis for English claims in the New World.

JOHN CABOT, OR GIOVANNI CABOTO, WAS AN ITALIAN, LIKE CHRISTOPHER COLUMBUS, OR CRISTOFORO COLOMBO. CABOT, TOO, WAS SEEKING A SHORT ROUTE TO THE INDIES.

1507

Inspired by news of voyages taken by Florentine merchant Amerigo Vespucci, who traveled to the New World around the turn of the sixteenth century, mapmaker Martin Waldseemüller names the new land America.

WALDSEEMÜLLER APPARENTLY HAD A CHANGE OF HEART ABOUT NAMING THE NEW WORLD AFTER VESPUCCI. IN A 1513 ATLAS HE CALLED THE NEW LAND TERRA INCOGNITA AND CREDITED COLUMBUS WITH ITS DISCOVERY. BUT BY THEN IT WAS TOO LATE, AND AMERICA IT WAS.

1513

Spanish exploration of mainland North America begins with Juan Ponce de León on the east coast of Florida. Among the others who will search for riches in the mainland are Hernando de Soto and Francisco Vásquez de Coronado.

"He also said that the lord of that country took his afternoon nap under a great tree on which were hung a great number of little golden bells, which put him to sleep as they swung in the air."

—An account of what a Pawnee guide told Coronado about a country of fabulous wealth. The fabled land was never found, and the guide was killed.

THE CONQUISTADORES, WHO EXPLORED THE LAND THAT IS TODAY THE UNITED STATES, FOUND LITTLE GOLD. BUT HERNÁN CORTÉS, WHO CONQUERED THE AZTECS IN MEXICO IN 1521, AND FRANCISCO PIZARRO, WHO CONQUERED THE INCAS IN PERU IN THE 1530S, FOUND TONS OF PRECIOUS METAL TO SHIP BACK TO SPAIN.

1524

Sailing for the French, Italian explorer Giovanni da Verrazano explores the east coast of North America, including New York harbor, searching for a passage to the Indies.

1534

French explorer Jacques Cartier makes the first of three voyages to North America.

AUGUST 10 IS THE FEAST DAY OF SAINT LAWRENCE, A ROMAN MARTYR WHO WAS PUT ON A GRILL AND ROASTED ALIVE. WHEN CARTIER SAILED INTO A WELL-PROTECTED HARBOR ON AUGUST 10, 1535, HE NAMED IT AFTER THE SAINT, AND FROM THENCE CAME THE NAMES OF THE GULF, THE RIVER, AND THE MOUNTAIN RANGE.

1565

At the direction of Philip II of Spain, Gen. Pedro Menéndez de Avilés establishes the first permanent European settlement in North America: Saint Augustine in Florida.

> *"The general marched up to the cross, followed by all who accompanied him, and there they kneeled and embraced the cross."*
>
> —Chaplain Francisco López de Mendoza Grajales, describing General Menéndez in the founding ceremony

1585–87

Sir Walter Raleigh, a favorite of Queen Elizabeth of England, sponsors two efforts to establish an English settlement on Roanoke Island. Most of the first group of settlers return to England; the second group, composed of more than one hundred men, women, and children, disappears and becomes known as the lost colony.

> "Croatoan"
>
> —Word carved on a post at the lost colony, thought to indicate a nearby island to which settlers had gone. But they were never found.

John White, governor of the second group on Roanoke Island, sailed to England soon after the colony was established to get supplies. Conflict between England and Spain prevented him from returning for more than two years. By then the colony, including his daughter and granddaughter, had disappeared.

1607

Three ships from England, the *Susan Constant*, the *Discovery*, and the *Godspeed*, enter Chesapeake Bay and sail up the James River. The passengers, some one hundred men, found Jamestown, Virginia, the first permanent English settlement in America.

> *"There was no talk, no hope, no work, but dig gold, wash gold, refine gold, load gold."*
>
> —JOHN SMITH, a leader of the Jamestown settlement, who managed to convince the colonists that since there was no gold, they should plant crops

1608

Juan Martinez de Montoya, a Spanish conquistador, establishes a settlement at Santa Fe. In 1610, at the order of Philip III, Santa Fe will become the capital of the province of New Mexico.

1608

Samuel de Champlain sails up the Saint Lawrence River and founds Quebec.

1609

Henry Hudson, sailing for the Dutch, explores the river that will bear his name.

1612

John Rolfe plants tobacco seeds in Jamestown, starting the colonists on their way to a successful commercial venture. By 1630 Virginia will be exporting well over a million pounds of tobacco a year.

Rolfe's 1614 marriage to Pocahontas, daughter of the powerful Powhatan, began a truce between Virginia settlers and Indians, but warfare broke out again in 1622 when an Indian attack left nearly a third of the colonists in Virginia dead.

Pocahontas

1619

The Virginia House of Burgesses, its members chosen by freemen in the colony, convenes at Jamestown and becomes the first elected assembly in America.

> *"The most convenient place we could find to sit in was the choir of the church. . . . But forasmuch as men's affairs do little prosper where God's service is neglected, . . . a prayer was said by Mr. Bucke, the*

minister, that it would please God to guide and sanctify all our proceedings."

—John Pory, secretary of the House of Burgesses

1619

Some twenty Africans, brought to Jamestown on a Dutch ship, are sold to colonists, most to work in tobacco fields.

The signing of the Mayflower Compact

1620

Pilgrims sail aboard the *Mayflower* from England to the New World, dropping anchor off Cape Cod. After forty-one men aboard the ship sign the Mayflower Compact, a plan for governance, the Pilgrims go ashore.

"Being thus arrived in a good harbor, and brought safe to land, they fell upon their knees and blessed the God of Heaven who had brought them over the fast and furious ocean, and delivered them from all the

perils and miseries thereof, again to set their feet on the firm and stable earth, their proper element."

—WILLIAM BRADFORD, governor of Plymouth Colony

OF THE 102 *MAYFLOWER* PASSENGERS 52, OR 53 PERHAPS, WERE PROTESTANT DISSENTERS WHO WANTED TO SEPARATE FROM THE CHURCH OF ENGLAND. THE OTHERS, WHOM BRADFORD CALLED "STRANGERS," HAD NO APPARENT QUARREL WITH THE CHURCH. MEMBERS OF BOTH GROUPS WERE BRAVE, SUFFERED GREATLY, AND ARE COMMONLY CALLED PILGRIMS.

1621

The Pilgrims celebrate the autumn harvest, feasting on turkey, duck, and venison with Indians of the Wampanoag nation.

"*Our harvest being gotten in, . . . many of the Indians [came] amongst us, and among the rest their greatest King Massasoit, with some ninety men, whom for three days we entertained and feasted.*"

—EDWARD WINSLOW, a *Mayflower* passenger

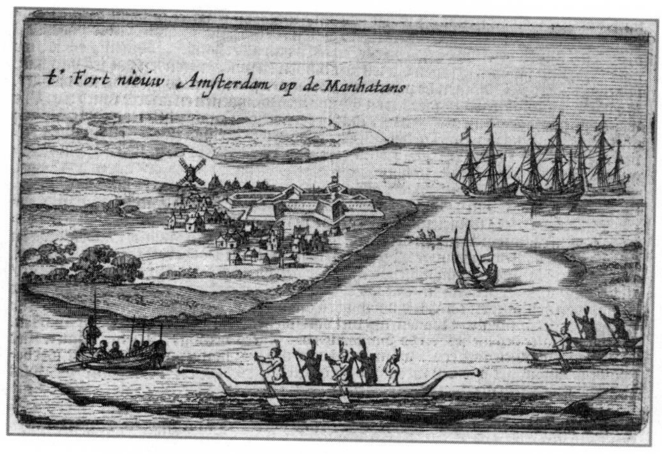

NEW AMSTERDAM (MANHATTAN), ABOUT 1626

1625

To protect their claim to lands they call New Netherland, the Dutch establish the settlement of New Amsterdam on Manhattan Island.

> *"They have purchased the Island Manhattes from the Indians for the value of 60 guilders."*
>
> —PIETER SCHAGEN, Dutch West India Company official, 1626

1630

John Winthrop and Puritan followers arrive from England and establish the Massachusetts Bay Colony, where they hope to create a pure and godly community. In the decade ahead thousands will follow in the Great Migration.

> *"He shall make us a praise and glory* [so] *that men shall say of succeeding* [colonies], *'May the Lord make it like that of New England.' For we must*

consider that we shall be as a city upon a hill. The eyes of all people are upon us."

—John Winthrop, Puritan leader

Nearly two thirds of the colonists at Jamestown died in the first year. Half those in Plymouth died during the Pilgrims' first winter there. The Puritans, better organized, had a better survival rate. Still, one of every five perished during their first year in America.

1634

Under the sponsorship of Lord Baltimore, who wants to create a place where Catholics can worship, some 150 Catholics and Protestants sail aboard the *Ark* and the *Dove* to Maryland.

"*The soil . . . is excellent so that we cannot set down a foot, but tread on strawberries, raspberries, fallen mulberry vines, acorns, walnuts, [and] sassafras.*"

—Father Andrew White

1635

Massachusetts congregations move into the Connecticut River valley. A group headed by Puritan minister Thomas Hooker will found Hartford the next year.

1636

Roger Williams is expelled from Massachusetts for his beliefs. He flees to Narragansett Bay and, in a few years, establishes the colony of Rhode Island, where Protestants, Jews, and Catholics are all free to worship.

"True civility and Christianity may both flourish in a state or kingdom, notwithstanding the permission of divers and contrary consciences, either of Jew or Gentile."

—Roger Williams

1636

Puritans in the Massachusetts Bay Colony found Harvard College.

"After God had carried us safe to New England, and we had builded our houses, provided necessaries for our livelihood, reared convenient places for God's worship, and settled the civil government: One of the next things we longed for, and looked after was to advance learning, and perpetuate it to posterity."

—Members of Harvard's first board of overseers

The first president of Harvard, Henry Dunster, set forth rules and precepts for the school. Every student had to write and speak Latin, diligently attend lectures, and "be plainly instructed, and earnestly pressed to consider well, [that] the main end of his life and studies is, to know God and Jesus Christ which is eternal life."

1637

After Pequot Indians kill two Englishmen, war breaks out between Pequots and New England settlers. Colonists, acting with Mohegan and Narragansett allies, attack and burn a Pequot village, killing hundreds.

1638

Anne Hutchinson, a religious dissenter, is ordered out of Massachusetts.

> *"Mrs. Hutchinson, the sentence of the court you hear is that you are banished from out of our jurisdiction as being a woman not fit for our society, and are to be imprisoned till the court shall send you away."*
>
> —Governor John Winthrop

Anne Hutchinson was the mother of fifteen children, three of whom died in England before she moved to Massachusetts. When she was banished, she moved with her children to Narragansett Bay, where her husband, William, and some friends had established a new settlement. After William died, Anne, in her early fifties, moved to Long Island Sound. There she and five of her children were killed by Indians.

1638

Swedish settlers aboard the *Kalmar Nyckel* and the *Fogel Grip* establish the colony of New Sweden in the Delaware River valley.

1642

Sir William Berkeley arrives in Jamestown. During two terms as governor he will persuade members of England's elite families to move to Virginia.

"A small sum of money will enable a younger brother to erect a flourishing family in a new world; and add more strength, wealth and honor to his native country, than thousands did before."

—SIR WILLIAM BERKELEY, explaining the advantages of Virginia to younger sons, who had no hope of inheriting their families' fortunes

1664

When an English naval force sails into New Amsterdam's harbor, New Netherland passes into English hands. It is divided into two parts, which are given the names New York and New Jersey. New Jersey will subsequently be divided into two parts, East and West Jersey.

THE COLONY OF NEW SWEDEN, OR DELAWARE, WHICH HAD BECOME PART OF NEW NETHERLAND, ALSO PASSED INTO ENGLISH HANDS IN 1664. THE DUKE OF YORK SUBSEQUENTLY GRANTED IT TO WILLIAM PENN, BUT IT HAD ITS OWN LEGISLATURE AND RETAINED A LARGE MEASURE OF AUTONOMY.

1670

English immigrants from Barbados arrive in the Carolina Colony, bringing at least one enslaved African with them. The sugarcane they have been growing in the West Indies does not flourish in the Carolina climate, but in the 1690s rice, another plantation crop, will be successfully introduced.

1675–76

Fighting between New England colonists and Indians led by Metacom, also known as King Philip, kills hundreds of colonists and thousands of Indians before Metacom himself is captured and killed.

Metacom was the son of Massasoit, who helped the Pilgrims.

1676

Nathaniel Bacon, convinced that Sir William Berkeley, the royal governor of Virginia, is providing colonists insufficient protection against Indians, leads a rebellion and burns Jamestown. The rebellion ends when Bacon becomes sick and dies.

1679

New Hampshire, which has been part of Massachusetts, becomes a separate royal province.

1681

William Penn, wishing to establish a community that reflects Quaker ideals of peace and tolerance, founds Pennsylvania. He resolves to deal justly with Indians.

> *"There is one great God and power that hath made the world and all things therein, to whom you, and I, and all people owe their being and well-being, and to whom you and I must one day give an account for all that we have done in the world. . . . Now this great God has been pleased to make me concerned in your part of the world; . . . but I desire to enjoy it with*

your love and consent, that we may always live together as neighbors and friends."

—WILLIAM PENN, writing to the Lenape nation

PENN ADVISED HIS CHILDREN TO CULTIVATE THE VIRTUES OF HUMILITY, PATIENCE, MERCY, GENEROSITY, JUSTICE, GRATITUDE, DILIGENCE, AND FRUGALITY. "HAVE AN HOLY AWE UPON YOUR MINDS TO AVOID THAT WHICH IS EVIL," HE TOLD THEM, "AND A STRICT CARE TO EMBRACE AND DO THAT WHICH IS GOOD."

WILLIAM PENN

1682

French explorer René-Robert Cavelier, Sieur de La Salle, travels the Mississippi River to the Gulf of Mexico. He names the entire river basin Louisiana in honor of Louis XIV and claims it for France.

1692

In Salem, Massachusetts, six men and fourteen women are executed for witchcraft. Nineteen are hanged, and one is pressed to death.

> *"An army of devils is horribly broke in upon the place which is the center."*
>
> —Cotton Mather, Puritan minister

Mather entered Harvard at age eleven, learned seven languages, published more than four hundred books, and was the father of fifteen children, only two of whom survived him. He saw witchcraft as a grave moral threat, but others at the time knew that great injustice was being done.

> *"Ages will not wear off that reproach and those stains which these things will leave behind them upon our land."*
>
> —Thomas Brattle, Boston merchant

1699

Williamsburg becomes the capital of Virginia.

Virginians decided to move their capital to Williamsburg after the statehouse in Jamestown was destroyed by fire four times: in 1655, around 1660, in 1676, and in 1698.

1702

East Jersey and West Jersey, under English control, are united into a single colony.

1710

Thousands of German immigrants arrive in America, to be followed by tens of thousands more, many of them indentured servants.

> *"People come from the city of Philadelphia and other places . . . and go on board the newly arrived ship . . . and select among the healthy persons such as they deem suitable for their business, and bargain with them how long they will serve for their passage money, which most of them are still in debt for."*
>
> —Gottlieb Mittelberger, who was not indentured, describing the fate of some of his fellow immigrants

---

ACCORDING TO THE 2000 CENSUS, NEARLY FORTY-THREE MILLION AMERICANS TRACE THEIR ANCESTRY TO GERMANY. THAT IS MORE THAN TO ANY OTHER NATION, INCLUDING ENGLAND.

1712

Carolina divides into North Carolina, where small farms prevail, and South Carolina, a land of rice plantations.

1714

Facing economic hardship and religious oppression, the Scots-Irish begin to emigrate to America in large numbers. They come to New England, then Pennsylvania. Many will move on to settle the frontier.

"There are now seven ships at Belfast that are carrying off about 1,000 passengers thither."

—Archbishop Boulter, Primate of Ireland, on departures for America

---

Famous Scots-Irish Americans associated with the frontier: Andrew Jackson, Davy Crockett, Sam Houston—and John Wayne.

1723

Benjamin Franklin, a seventeen-year-old runaway apprentice, arrives in Philadelphia. As printer, publisher, author, inventor, scientist, philosopher, and statesman, he will shape his city and his country.

"Strive to be the greatest man in your country, and you may be disappointed; strive to be the best, and you may succeed."

—Benjamin Franklin

Benjamin Franklin in about 1766

1730s and 1740s

In what will become known as the Great Awakening, a series of religious revivals sweep across the colonies.

> "*As grace is at first from God, so it is continually from him, and is maintained by him, as much as light in the atmosphere is all day long from the sun.*"
>
> —JONATHAN EDWARDS, New England clergyman

BENJAMIN FRANKLIN, GOING TO HEAR GEORGE WHITEFIELD, FAMED ENGLISH PREACHER OF THE GREAT AWAKENING, RESOLVED NOT TO CONTRIBUTE TO WHITEFIELD'S CAUSE. BUT IN THE END, FRANKLIN WROTE, "I EMPTIED MY POCKET WHOLLY INTO THE COLLECTOR'S DISH, GOLD AND ALL."

1733

British philanthropist James Oglethorpe leads a band of settlers to Georgia to create a colony intended to be a haven for the poor and oppressed.

WITH THE FORMATION OF GEORGIA THE OUTLINES WERE IN PLACE FOR THIRTEEN BRITISH COLONIES: FOUR IN NEW ENGLAND (MASSACHUSETTS, CONNECTICUT, RHODE ISLAND, AND NEW HAMPSHIRE), FOUR MIDDLE COLONIES (NEW YORK, NEW JERSEY, DELAWARE, AND PENNSYLVANIA), AND FIVE COLONIES TO THE SOUTH (VIRGINIA, MARYLAND, NORTH CAROLINA, SOUTH CAROLINA, AND GEORGIA).

VERMONT, ITS LANDS CLAIMED BY NEW YORK AND NEW HAMPSHIRE, DECLARED ITSELF TO BE A FREE AND INDEPENDENT REPUBLIC IN 1777 AND MAINTAINED THAT STATUS UNTIL IT ENTERED THE UNION AS THE FOURTEENTH STATE IN 1791.

MAINE WAS PART OF MASSACHUSETTS UNTIL 1820, WHEN IT ENTERED THE UNION AS A SEPARATE STATE.

1735

Printer John Peter Zenger, on trial for "seditious libel" because his newspaper has criticized the Crown-appointed governor of New York, is found innocent.

> "*The question before the court and you gentlemen of the jury is not of small nor private concern, it is not the cause of a poor printer, nor of* New York *alone, which you are now trying:* No! *It may in its consequence affect every freeman that lives under a* British *government on the main of* America. *It is the best cause. It is the cause of liberty.*"
>
> —ANDREW HAMILTON, Zenger's defense attorney

TWO

CREATING A NATION

1754–63

In a conflict that will be known as the French and Indian War, British forces, fighting with colonists at their side, defeat the French and their Indian allies. Their victory gives the British control of Canada as well as lands east of the Mississippi River and west of the Appalachian Mountains.

IN AN EARLY BATTLE OF THE FRENCH AND INDIAN WAR, FORCES UNDER GEN. EDWARD BRADDOCK SUFFERED A GREAT DEFEAT NEAR FORT DUQUESNE. THE GENERAL AND HUNDREDS OF HIS MEN WERE KILLED, BUT SURVIVING AND ACQUITTING HIMSELF BRAVELY WAS TWENTY-THREE-YEAR-OLD GEORGE WASHINGTON, WHO HAD TWO HORSES SHOT OUT FROM UNDER HIM AND FOUR MUSKET BALLS GO THROUGH HIS CLOTHES.

> "As I *have heard . . . a circumstantial account of my death and dying speech,* I *take this early opportunity of contradicting both, and of assuring you that* I *now exist and appear in the land of the living.*"
>
> —GEORGE WASHINGTON, to his brother

1763

The British government forbids colonists from moving west of the Appalachian Mountains, but colonists ignore the edict and go anyway.

1765

The British try to raise money with the Stamp Act, a tax on colonists that is met with protest and boycott.

> *"If this be treason, make the most of it."*
>
> —Patrick Henry, denouncing King George and the Stamp Act

GROUPS CALLING THEMSELVES THE SONS OF LIBERTY ORGANIZED SECRETLY TO OPPOSE THE STAMP ACT AND FOMENTED PROTESTS THAT SOMETIMES TURNED VIOLENT. IN BOSTON MOBS RANSACKED AND BURNED THE HOUSE OF THE AMERICAN LIEUTENANT GOVERNOR OF MASSACHUSETTS, THOMAS HUTCHINSON, WHO WAS SUSPECTED OF BEING SYMPATHETIC TO THE BRITISH. HE WAS THE GREAT-GREAT-GRANDSON OF ANNE HUTCHINSON.

1766

Parliament repeals the Stamp Act but passes the Declaratory Act, which insists on Parliament's right to make laws that are binding on the colonies "in all cases whatsoever."

1767

The Townshend Acts, a new British effort to tax Americans, spur protest and boycott.

> *"First strip a person naked, then heat the tar until it is thin, and pour it upon the naked flesh, or rub it over with a tar brush. . . . After which, sprinkle*

decently upon the tar, whilst it is yet warm, as many feathers as will stick to it."

—Instructions for tarring and feathering, a technique sometimes used by colonists to intimidate British officials and sympathizers

1768

"The Liberty Song," America's first patriotic song, is published.

Then join hand in hand, brave Americans all!
By uniting we stand, by dividing we fall!

—JOHN DICKINSON, supporter of the colonial cause

THE LIBERTY SONG," SELDOM PERFORMED TODAY, WAS SUNG BY THE CHOIR OF DICKINSON COLLEGE (NAMED AFTER JOHN DICKINSON) ON NOVEMBER 9, 2001, AS A TRIBUTE TO THOSE WHO LOST THEIR LIVES ON SEPTEMBER 11, 2001.

1769

Father Junípero Serra, sent by the government of Spain, arrives at San Diego, where he founds the first of California's missions. Dedicated to converting the Indians of California to Catholicism, he will establish eight other missions in California before he dies in 1784.

"About halfway [on the journey to San Diego], the valleys and banks of rivulets began to be delightful. We found vines of a large size, and in some cases

quite loaded with grapes; we also found an abundance of roses, which appeared to be like those of Castile."

—Father Junípero Serra

1770

Facing a Boston mob armed with clubs, British troops fire on the crowd and kill five.

Sam Adams described the Boston shootings as "bloody butchery" and helped fix the event in the American mind as the Boston Massacre, but his second cousin John Adams defended the British troops in court. A captain and six soldiers were acquitted. Two British soldiers were found guilty of manslaughter and sentenced to branding on their thumbs.

"Facts are stubborn things, and whatever may be our wishes, our inclinations, or the dictums of our passions, they cannot alter the state of facts and evidence."

—John Adams

1770

The British parliament repeals the Townshend Acts, except for the tax on tea.

1773

The British grant a tea monopoly to the East India Company, inspiring Bostonians, disguised as Indians, to board ships in Boston Harbor and dump tea into the bay.

BOSTON TEA PARTY

"This destruction of the tea is so bold, so daring, so firm, intrepid and inflexible, and it must have so important consequences, and so lasting, that I can't but consider it as an epocha in history."

—JOHN ADAMS

John and Abigail Adams in 1766

1774

To punish colonists, Bostonians in particular, the British parliament passes laws that the colonists call the Intolerable Acts. Among other provisions these acts close the port of Boston and permit British troops to be quartered in private homes.

1774

The First Continental Congress meets in Philadelphia. It declares Parliament has violated colonists' rights and urges preparations for defense.

> "*To these grievous acts and measures, Americans cannot submit.*"
>
> —First Continental Congress

1775

Daniel Boone and a band of thirty blaze the Wilderness Road across the Appalachian Mountains and through the Cumberland Gap.

"We proceeded with all possible expedition until we came within fifteen miles of where Boonesborough *now stands, and where we were fired upon by a party of* Indians, *that killed two, and wounded two. . . . Three days after, we were fired upon again, and had two men killed, and three wounded. Afterward we proceeded on to* Kentucky River *without opposition."*

—Daniel Boone, frontiersman

1775

Virginia's leaders vote to raise an armed militia.

"Is life so dear, or peace so sweet, as to be purchased at the price of chains and slavery? Forbid it, Almighty God*! I know not what course others may take; but as for me, give me liberty or give me death!"*

—Patrick Henry, speaking to the Virginia legislature

1775

British troops, moving to seize a store of arms in Concord, Massachusetts, encounter militiamen at Lexington, and shooting breaks out, leaving eight colonists dead. A skirmish at North Bridge forces the British to retreat; by the time they make it back to Boston, 273 redcoats are killed, wounded, or missing.

"Stand your ground. Don't fire unless fired upon, but if they mean to have a war, let it begin here."

—Militia captain John Parker

On the night of April 18, 1775, both Paul Revere and William Dawes rode to sound the alarm that the redcoats were coming. They reached Lexington but then ran into a British patrol. Dawes turned back, and Revere was arrested, but Dr. Samuel Prescott, who had joined Revere and Dawes, made it to Concord and alerted the militia there.

1775

Ethan Allen and the Green Mountain Boys capture Fort Ticonderoga.

When a British officer demanded to know on what authority Allen was acting, legend has it that Allen replied, "In the name of the great Jehovah and the Continental Congress."

1775

The Second Continental Congress chooses George Washington to head the Continental army.

> "*I assure you, in the most solemn manner, that, so far from seeking this appointment I have used every endeavor in my power to avoid it, not only from my unwillingness to part with you and the family, but from a consciousness of its being a trust too great for my capacity. . . . But, as it has been a kind of destiny*

that has thrown me upon this service, I shall hope that my undertaking of it, is designed to answer some good purpose."

—George Washington, in a letter to Martha Washington

The Battle of Bunker Hill

1775

In what will become known as the Battle of Bunker Hill, the British attack American militiamen dug in on Breed's Hill and drive them off, but only after suffering more than one thousand casualties.

"I *wish [we] could sell them another hill at the same price."*

—American general Nathanael Greene

ALTHOUGH MOST OF THE FIGHTING TOOK PLACE ON BREED'S HILL, SOME ACTION DID OCCUR ON BUNKER HILL, THE NAME ASSOCIATED WITH THE BATTLE FROM THE BEGINNING. BOSTONIANS MAY HAVE FOUND IT EASIER TO REFER TO THE CONFLICT AS THE BATTLE OF BUNKER HILL, SINCE BREED'S HILL WAS NOT AS FAMILIAR A PLACE NAME AT THE TIME.

1776

Thomas Paine's essay *Common Sense* lays out the case for revolution.

> *"The period of debate is closed. Arms, as the last resource, decide the contest. . . . The blood of the slain, the weeping voice of nature cries,* 'TIS TIME TO PART."
>
> —THOMAS PAINE

TALK OF REVOLUTION LED ABIGAIL ADAMS TO TAKE UP THE SUBJECT OF WOMEN'S RIGHTS WITH HER HUSBAND, JOHN. ON MARCH 31, 1776, SHE WROTE TO HIM, "IN THE NEW CODE OF LAWS WHICH I SUPPOSE IT WILL BE NECESSARY FOR YOU TO MAKE I DESIRE YOU WOULD REMEMBER THE LADIES, AND BE MORE GENEROUS AND FAVORABLE TO THEM THAN YOUR ANCESTORS."

July 4, 1776

The Continental Congress formally approves the Declaration of Independence.

"We hold these truths to be self-evident, that all men are created equal, that they are endowed by their creator with certain unalienable rights, that among these are life, liberty and the pursuit of happiness."

—The Declaration of Independence

THE SIGNING OF THE DECLARATION OF INDEPENDENCE

ACCORDING TO JOHN ADAMS, IT WAS HIS IDEA THAT THOMAS JEFFERSON WRITE THE DECLARATION OF INDEPENDENCE. HE GAVE JEFFERSON THREE REASONS: "REASON FIRST: YOU ARE A VIRGINIAN AND A VIRGINIAN OUGHT TO APPEAR AT THE HEAD OF THIS BUSINESS. REASON SECOND: I AM OBNOXIOUS, SUSPECTED AND UNPOPULAR. YOU ARE VERY MUCH OTHERWISE. REASON THIRD: YOU CAN WRITE TEN TIMES BETTER THAN I CAN."

ADAMS THOUGHT THAT AMERICAN INDEPENDENCE OUGHT TO BE RECOGNIZED WITH "POMP AND PARADE . . . FROM THIS TIME FORWARD FOREVER MORE." BUT HE THOUGHT AMERICANS WOULD CELEBRATE ON JULY 2, THE DAY CONGRESS VOTED THAT THE COLONIES WERE INDEPENDENT, RATHER THAN ON JULY 4, WHEN THE DECLARATION WAS FORMALLY APPROVED.

1776

Sent behind enemy lines to gather information for George Washington, twenty-one-year-old Nathan Hale is captured by the British and hanged.

> "I *only regret that* I *have but one life to lose for my country.*"
>
> —Capt. Nathan Hale

1776

As Americans suffer early military defeats, Thomas Paine writes words to encourage them.

> *"These are the times that try men's souls. The summer soldier and the sunshine patriot will, in this crisis, shrink from the service of their country; but he that stands it* now, *deserves the love and thanks of man and woman."*
>
> —Thomas Paine, *The American Crisis*

GEORGE WASHINGTON CROSSING THE DELAWARE

1776–77

George Washington decides to go on the attack, crosses the Delaware River on Christmas night, and leads Americans to victory first at Trenton and then, in the New Year, at Princeton.

> *"Away, my dear colonel, and bring up the troops—the day is our own!"*
>
> —GEN. GEORGE WASHINGTON

THREE GROUPS OF AMERICAN FIGHTING MEN TRIED TO CROSS THE DELAWARE ON CHRISTMAS NIGHT, BUT ICE FORMING IN THE RIVER WAS TOO MUCH FOR TWO OF THEM. ONLY THE GROUP COMMANDED BY WASHINGTON MADE IT ACROSS.

1777

Congress adopts the Stars and Stripes.

> "*Resolved, that the flag of the thirteen* United States *be thirteen stripes, alternate red and white: that the* Union *be thirteen stars, white in a blue field, representing a new constellation.*"
>
> —Continental Congress

1777

The British defeat George Washington and his troops at Brandywine Creek and occupy Philadelphia.

1777

American forces defeat the British at Saratoga.

> "*We now become fully convinced they are not that contemptible enemy we had hitherto imagined them.*"
>
> —British lieutenant Thomas Anburey

1777

General Washington and his troops march to winter quarters at Valley Forge, where they will endure months of suffering and hardship.

> "*Under all those disadvantages no men ever show more spirit or prudence than ours. In my opinion nothing but virtue has kept our army together through this campaign.*"
>
> —Col. John Brooks, in a letter from Valley Forge

1778

Encouraged by the American victory at Saratoga and the diplomacy of Benjamin Franklin, in Paris as an American commissioner, France declares support for the American cause.

1781

The Articles of Confederation are ratified and become the governing framework for the thirteen states.

1781

With the help of a French fleet and troops, American forces under the command of General Washington defeat Gen. Charles Cornwallis and his forces at Yorktown, effectively ending the war.

> "*Oh God! It is all over.*"
>
> —British prime minister LORD NORTH, according to legend

1783

The Treaty of Paris formally ends the Revolutionary War.

> "*The citizens of America . . . are, from this period, to be considered as the actors on a most conspicuous theater, which seems to be peculiarly designated by Providence for the display of human greatness and felicity.*"
>
> —GEORGE WASHINGTON, *Circular to the States*

Thomas Jefferson

1786

The Virginia Statute for Religious Freedom, written by Thomas Jefferson and shepherded through the Virginia legislature by James Madison, becomes law.

> *"Be it therefore enacted by the General Assembly . . . that all men shall be free to profess, and by argument to maintain, their opinion in matters of religion."*
>
> —The Virginia Statute for Religious Freedom

At his request, Thomas Jefferson's tombstone identifies him as the author of the Declaration of Independence, the author of the Virginia Statute for Religious Freedom, and the father of the University of Virginia.

1786–87

Under the leadership of Daniel Shays, who served in the Revolutionary War, economically pressed farmers in Massachusetts engage in armed revolt. A hastily assembled militia crushes the rebellion, but the lawlessness encourages some to believe that the United States needs a stronger central government.

> *"For what have we been contending against the tyranny of Britain, to become the sacrifice of a lawless banditti?"*
>
> —ABIGAIL ADAMS

> *"I like a little rebellion now and then. It is like a storm in the atmosphere."*
>
> —THOMAS JEFFERSON

1787

The Confederation Congress passes the Northwest Ordinance, barring slavery in the lands north of the Ohio River and east of the Mississippi, determining how new states will be formed, and encouraging education.

> *"Religion, morality, and knowledge, being necessary to good government and the happiness of mankind, schools and the means of education shall forever be encouraged."*
>
> —The Northwest Ordinance

THREE YEARS BEFORE THE NORTHWEST ORDINANCE, A COMMITTEE HEADED BY THOMAS JEFFERSON RECOMMENDED THAT SEVENTEEN STATES BE created out of western lands, and suggested names for them, including Chersonesus, Sylvania, Assenisipia, Metropotamia, Polypotamia, and Pelisipia. The plan was not approved.

1787

Delegates meeting in Philadelphia create a new and stronger framework for government, the Constitution of the United States.

> *"We the people of the United States, in order to form a more perfect union, establish justice, insure domestic tranquility, provide for the common defense, promote the general welfare, and secure the blessings of liberty to ourselves and our posterity, do ordain and establish this Constitution for the United States of America."*
>
> —Preamble to the Constitution

The Constitutional Convention was supposed to start on May 14, 1787. James Madison, who, more than any other, shaped the convention's outcome, arrived eleven days early, on May 3. George Washington arrived on May 13. Largely owing to difficulties of travel, many delegates were late, and the convention did not get under way until May 25.

> "A *republic, if you can keep it.*"
>
> —Benjamin Franklin, on being asked by a woman what kind of government the convention had created

1787–88

John Jay, James Madison, and Alexander Hamilton write newspaper articles explaining the Constitution and building support for its ratification. Their essays will become known as the Federalist Papers.

JAMES MADISON

"This country and this people seem to have been made for each other."

—JOHN JAY, Federalist Paper No. 2

"They accomplished a revolution which has no parallel in the annals of human society. They reared the fabrics of governments which have no model on the face of the globe. They formed the design of a great Confederacy, which it is incumbent on their successors to improve and perpetuate."

—JAMES MADISON, Federalist Paper No. 14

"It seems to have been reserved to the people of this country, by their conduct and example, to decide the important question, whether societies of men are really capable or not of establishing good government from reflection and choice, or whether they are forever destined to depend for their political constitutions on accident and force."

—Alexander Hamilton, Federalist Paper No. 1

Alexander Hamilton

Born in poverty in the West Indies, Alexander Hamilton wrote about two thirds of the Federalist Papers. He had served as an aide to George Washington in the Revolutionary War and became, at age thirty-two, Washington's secretary of the treasury. At age forty-seven he was killed in a duel by then vice president Aaron Burr.

OPPOSING THE CONSTITUTION WERE ANTI-FEDERALISTS, WHO FEARED THAT A STRONG CENTRAL GOVERNMENT WOULD PUT AT RISK THE FREEDOMS THEY HAD JUST WON IN THE REVOLUTION.

"This constitution . . . squints toward monarchy, and does not this raise indignation in the breast of every true American?"

—PATRICK HENRY, arguing against the Constitution in the Virginia convention called to ratify it

1788

The Constitution, ratified by nine of the thirteen states, becomes law.

1789

Olaudah Equiano, a former slave, publishes his autobiography.

"Two of my wearied countrymen who were chained together . . . , preferring death to such a life of misery, somehow made through the nettings and jumped into the sea: immediately another quite dejected fellow . . . followed their example. . . . Two of the wretches were drowned, but they got the other, and afterwards flogged him unmercifully for thus attempting to prefer death to slavery."

—OLAUDAH EQUIANO, describing life on the slave ship that brought him across the Atlantic

EQUIANO'S AUTOBIOGRAPHY ENCOURAGED GROWING ANTISLAVERY SENTIMENT IN THE NORTH. BY THE TIME HIS BOOK WAS PUBLISHED, VERMONT, MASSACHUSETTS, AND NEW HAMPSHIRE HAD ABOLISHED SLAVERY. PENNSYLVANIA, RHODE ISLAND, AND CONNECTICUT HAD PROVIDED FOR A GRADUAL END. NEW YORK ENACTED GRADUAL EMANCIPATION IN 1799, AS DID NEW JERSEY IN 1804.

1789

George Washington is sworn in as the first president of the United States.

"I *walk on untrodden ground.*"
—President George Washington

Washington's inauguration at New York City's Federal Hall

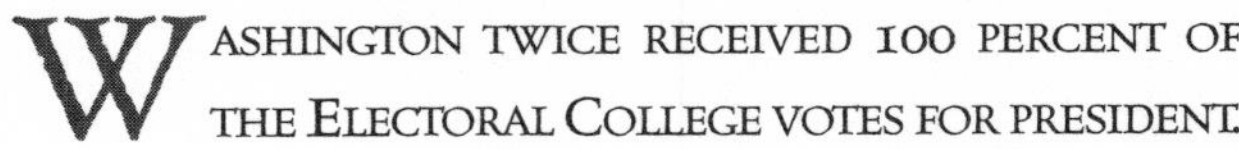

WASHINGTON TWICE RECEIVED 100 PERCENT OF THE ELECTORAL COLLEGE VOTES FOR PRESIDENT.

Franklin D. Roosevelt received the second-greatest percentage, 98.5 percent, in 1936. James Monroe was third, with 98.3 percent in 1820; Ronald Reagan fourth, with 97.6 percent in 1984; Richard Nixon fifth, with 96.7 percent in 1972.

1790

According to the first census, the United States has a population of 3,929,214. The number of slaves is 717,021.

1790

Samuel Slater opens a textile factory in Rhode Island, thus bringing the Industrial Revolution to America.

Slater learned the mechanics of textile manufacturing in an English mill. Because the British restricted emigration of persons with such knowledge, Slater described himself as a farmworker when he got on a ship bound for America in 1789.

1791

Congress passes a bill creating a national bank, although some think the action is unconstitutional. At the urging of Secretary of the Treasury Alexander Hamilton, who argues that creating a bank is among the powers implied by the Constitution, Washington will sign the bill.

1791

Vermont becomes the fourteenth state to join the Union.

1791

The first ten amendments to the Constitution, known as the Bill of Rights, are ratified by three fourths of the states and become part of the Constitution.

> *"Congress shall make no law respecting an establishment of religion, or prohibiting the free exercise thereof; or abridging the freedom of speech, or of the press; or the right of the people peaceably to assemble, and to petition the government for a redress of grievances."*
>
> —The First Amendment

JAMES MADISON, AUTHOR OF THE BILL OF RIGHTS, ORIGINALLY DREW UP TWELVE AMENDMENTS, BUT ONE, ABOUT THE NUMBER OF CONGRESSMEN, WAS NEVER RATIFIED, AND A SECOND, ABOUT CONGRESSIONAL PAY, WAS NOT RATIFIED UNTIL 1992, MORE THAN TWO HUNDRED YEARS AFTER IT WAS PROPOSED.

1792

Kentucky becomes the fifteenth state to join the Union.

1793

Eli Whitney, a recent college graduate, visits a Georgia plantation and invents the cotton gin, making cotton production more profitable, which in turn leads to a dramatic expansion of slavery in the South.

WHITNEY ALSO PLAYED AN IMPORTANT ROLE IN THE HISTORY OF MASS PRODUCTION BY PIONEERING THE MANUFACTURE OF GUNS WITH INTERCHANGEABLE PARTS. RIFLES TURNED OUT IN ACCORDANCE WITH THIS SYSTEM WERE USED IN THE CIVIL WAR—A CONFLICT THAT THE COTTON GIN HELPED BRING ABOUT.

1793

Thomas Jefferson, George Washington's secretary of state, retires from the cabinet, where he has been almost constantly at odds with Secretary of the Treasury Alexander Hamilton.

THOMAS JEFFERSON AND ALEXANDER HAMILTON HAD DIVERGENT WORLDVIEWS, WITH HAMILTON FAVORING A STRONG CENTRAL GOVERNMENT AND JEFFERSON FEARING IT. FROM THESE DIFFERENT PHILOSOPHIES POLITICAL PARTIES WERE FORMED, AND A DEBATE WAS SET IN MOTION THAT IS ONGOING TODAY.

1794

When mobs in Pennsylvania threaten a rebellion over a federal excise tax on whiskey, President George Washington, determined to put down what he sees as a challenge to constitutional government, leads a militia of thirteen thousand men against the rebels. They disperse as the army approaches.

Washington sending troops to put down the Whiskey Rebellion

> *"When we call to mind the gracious indulgence of heaven by which the American people became a nation; when we survey the general prosperity of our country, and look forward to the riches, power, and happiness to which it seems destined, with the deepest regret do I announce to you that during your recess some of the citizens of the United States have been found capable of insurrection."*
>
> —President Washington, reporting to Congress about the late rebellion

1794

At the orders of President George Washington, who is trying to avoid war, John Jay, the chief justice of the Supreme Court, concludes a treaty with the British. It proves to be unpopular, but Washington stands by it, and in 1795 the Senate ratifies it. War is avoided, at least for the time being.

1796

Tennessee becomes the sixteenth state to join the Union.

1796

President George Washington, deciding to retire after his second term, issues his farewell address. In it he urges Americans to stay independent from other nations and to love their own.

> *"Citizens, by birth or choice, of a common country, that country has a right to concentrate your affections. The name of American, which belongs to you . . . , must always exalt the just pride of patriotism more than any appellation derived from local discriminations."*
>
> —GEORGE WASHINGTON

EVERY YEAR SINCE 1896 WASHINGTON'S BIRTHDAY HAS BEEN MARKED BY A READING OF HIS FAREWELL ADDRESS ON THE FLOOR OF THE U.S. SENATE.

1796

In the first contested presidential election, John Adams, representing the Federalists, the party of strong central government, defeats Thomas Jefferson, representing the Democratic-Republicans, who view a strong federal government as a threat to the rights of states and individuals. Jefferson receives the second-highest number of electoral votes and will become vice president.

1798

As the United States fights an undeclared naval war with France, the Federalist Congress passes and President John Adams signs the Alien and Sedition Acts. It becomes a crime to criticize the government.

AMONG THOSE JAILED UNDER THE SEDITION ACT WAS ANTI-FEDERALIST CONGRESSMAN MATTHEW LYON OF VERMONT, WHO CRITICIZED PRESIDENT ADAMS FOR HIS "UNBOUNDED THIRST FOR RIDICULOUS POMP, FOOLISH ADULATION, AND SELFISH AVARICE." LYON CAMPAIGNED FOR HIS CONGRESSIONAL SEAT FROM JAIL AND WAS REELECTED.

1798

Thomas Jefferson and James Madison, acting in concert, get resolutions passed by the state legislatures of Kentucky and Virginia denouncing the Alien and Sedition Acts. The Kentucky and Virginia Resolutions advance the idea that the Constitution is a compact agreed upon by the states and that the states have the power to say when Congress has overreached.

> *"The General Assembly doth particularly protest against the palpable and alarming infractions of the Constitution, in the two late cases of the 'Alien and Sedition Acts' passed at the last session of Congress."*
>
> —Virginia Resolution

1800

Washington, D.C., becomes the capital of the United States.

Washington, D.C., is the ninth city to serve as the seat of government for the United States. The others are Philadelphia, Pennsylvania; Baltimore, Maryland; Lancaster, Pennsylvania; York, Pennsylvania; Princeton, New Jersey; Annapolis, Maryland; Trenton, New Jersey; and New York City.

U.S. Capitol in 1800

1800

President John Adams and his wife, Abigail, are the first to live in what he calls the "President's House."

> *"I pray heaven to bestow the best of blessings on this house and all that shall hereafter inhabit it. May none but honest and wise men ever rule under this roof."*
>
> —President John Adams, writing to Abigail

THREE

A HOUSE DIVIDED

1800

In a bitterly contested election John Adams and Thomas Jefferson compete for the presidency for a second time. Jefferson wins seventy-three electoral votes to Adams's sixty-five, but Jefferson's vice presidential candidate, Aaron Burr, wins seventy-three as well, and the election has to be decided by the House of Representatives. Jefferson is elected, and Burr becomes vice president.

THE ORIGINAL CONSTITUTIONAL PLAN OF HAVING EACH ELECTOR CAST TWO VOTES, WITH THE WINNER BECOMING PRESIDENT AND THE RUNNER-UP VICE PRESIDENT, DID NOT WORK ONCE CANDIDATES FOR THE TWO OFFICES BEGAN RUNNING TOGETHER ON A PARTY TICKET. TO AVOID A REPEAT OF THE ELECTION OF 1800, THE TWELFTH AMENDMENT, PROVIDING FOR SEPARATE VOTES FOR PRESIDENT AND VICE PRESIDENT, WAS ADDED TO THE CONSTITUTION.

> *"We are all Republicans, we are all Federalists."*
>
> —THOMAS JEFFERSON, binding up partisan wounds in his first inaugural address

1801

President Jefferson sends a naval squadron to North Africa, where Barbary Coast states are preying on American ships. America's first foreign conflict will last four years and end inconclusively, but provide occasion for heroism.

When Tripoli captured the frigate *Philadelphia*, American naval commanders were determined not to let the ship become part of Tripoli's navy. Lt. Stephen Decatur led a dangerous nighttime raid that burned the ship.

"*The most bold and daring act of the age.*"

—Adm. Horatio Nelson, on the burning of the *Philadelphia*

1803

In *Marbury v. Madison* the Supreme Court, led by Chief Justice John Marshall, asserts the power of the Court to decide if laws passed by Congress are constitutional.

"*A law repugnant to the Constitution is void.*"

—John Marshall, *Marbury v. Madison*

1803

Ohio enters the Union as the seventeenth state.

1803

Under President Jefferson's leadership the United States purchases the Louisiana Territory from France for $15 million and doubles the country's size.

"*Let the land rejoice, for you have bought Louisiana for a song.*"

—Gen. Horatio Gates, to President Thomas Jefferson

JEFFERSON WORRIED THAT THERE WAS NO CONSTITUTIONAL PROVISION FOR THE UNITED STATES TO ACQUIRE FOREIGN LAND, BUT AMENDING THE CONSTITUTION MIGHT GIVE THE FRENCH TIME TO CHANGE THEIR MIND. "THE LESS WE SAY ABOUT CONSTITUTIONAL DIFFICULTIES RESPECTING LOUISIANA THE BETTER," HE WROTE TO JAMES MADISON.

1804–06

At President Jefferson's direction Meriwether Lewis and William Clark lead the Corps of Discovery to explore the American West.

> *"In obedience to your orders we have penetrated the continent of* North America *to the* Pacific *Ocean."*
>
> —Meriwether Lewis, drafting a report to President Jefferson as he returned to St. Louis

Meriwether Lewis and William Clark

The only woman in the Corps of Discovery was Sacagawea, a Shoshone, who served as interpreter and whose "fortitude and resolution" were noted in one of Captain Lewis's journal entries. She carried her infant son from North Dakota to the Pacific Ocean and back.

1807

Robert Fulton's steamship the *Clermont* travels up the Hudson River.

> *"The power of propelling boats by steam is now fully proved."*
>
> —Robert Fulton

Fulton's steamboat

1808

Importing slaves into the United States becomes illegal.

"And when they shall ask, in time to come, saying, What mean the lessons, the psalms, the prayers and the praises in the worship of this day? let us answer them, by saying, the Lord, on the day of which this is the anniversary, abolished the trade which dragged your fathers from their native country, and sold them as bondmen in the United States of America."

—Rev. Absalom Jones

1808

Tecumseh, a Shawnee chief, and his brother, the Prophet, begin to organize Indians east of the Mississippi into a confederacy to oppose further white incursions.

"Back whence they came, upon a trail of blood, they must be driven! Back—aye, back into the great water whose accursed waves brought them to our shores! Burn their dwellings—destroy their stock—slay their wives and children, that the very breed may perish. War now! War always!"

—Tecumseh

1808

James Madison is elected president of the United States.

1811

Waiting until Tecumseh is away, William Henry Harrison leads a force of one thousand to the headquarters of the Shawnee chief's confederacy. In what will become known as the Battle of Tippecanoe, the Shawnees attack Harrison and his men, who, in turn, burn the Indian village.

1812

Louisiana enters the Union as the eighteenth state.

1812

With western and southern congressmen denouncing the British for inciting Indian unrest and seizing U.S. sailors, James Madison sends a war message to Congress. On June 18 the United States declares war.

> *"What are we to gain by war? What are we not to lose by peace?—commerce, character, a nation's best treasure, honor!"*
>
> —Henry Clay, Speaker of the House of Representatives

1813

The British capture the American frigate *Chesapeake* outside Boston Harbor.

> *"Don't give up the ship!"*
>
> —*Chesapeake* captain James Lawrence, according to tradition, just before he died

1813

American naval commander Oliver Hazard Perry wins a victory on Lake Erie.

> *"We have met the enemy and they are ours."*
>
> —Oliver Hazard Perry

1813

Francis Cabot Lowell and several partners build a textile factory in Massachusetts that not only spins cotton thread but weaves it into cloth.

1814

The British burn Washington.

> *"Of the Senate house, the president's palace, the barracks, the dockyard, etc. nothing could be seen, except heaps of smoking ruins."*
>
> —British lieutenant GEORGE GLEIG

THE CAPITOL AFTER THE BURNING OF WASHINGTON

1814

After the British bombard Baltimore's Fort McHenry, Francis Scott Key, detained on a British ship, sees the American flag still flying.

O say can you see, by the dawn's early light,
What so proudly we hailed at the twilight's last gleaming,
Whose broad stripes and bright stars through the perilous fight
O'er the ramparts we watched were so gallantly streaming?

And the rocket's red glare, the bomb bursting in air,
Gave proof through the night that our flag was still
there,
O say does that star-spangled banner yet wave
O'er the land of the free and the home of the brave?

—Francis Scott Key, "The Star-Spangled Banner," original version

1815

Andrew Jackson leads American troops to an overwhelming victory over the British in the Battle of New Orleans. The British suffer more than two thousand casualties, the Americans fewer than one hundred, and Jackson becomes a national hero.

"ALMOST INCREDIBLE VICTORY!!!"

—*Daily National Intelligencer*

Andrew Jackson at the Battle of New Orleans

THE TREATY OF GHENT, WHICH ENDED THE WAR OF 1812, WAS ACTUALLY SIGNED BEFORE THE BATTLE OF NEW ORLEANS, BUT BECAUSE OF SLOW COMMUNICATIONS NEITHER AMERICAN NOR BRITISH FORCES KNEW ABOUT IT.

1815

Capt. Stephen Decatur sails with a naval squadron to the coast of North Africa and convinces countries along the Barbary Coast to end their piracy against American ships.

1816

James Monroe is elected president of the United States.

1816

Indiana enters the Union as the nineteenth state.

1817

Mississippi enters the Union as the twentieth state.

1818

Illinois enters the Union as the twenty-first state.

1819

After American troops led by Andrew Jackson invade Florida, the United States and Spain conclude a treaty that concedes the territory to the United States.

1819

Alabama enters the Union as the twenty-second state.

1820

To quiet the furor created when Missouri, where slavery exists, requests statehood, members of Congress agree to the Missouri Compromise, which provides for the admission of Missouri as a slave state and the prohibition of slavery in all other territory north of latitude 36°30'. In order to keep Missouri's admission from upsetting the balance of free and slave states, agreement is reached also to admit the free state of Maine.

1820

Maine enters the Union as the twenty-third state.

1821

Missouri enters the Union as the twenty-fourth state.

> *"The Missouri question . . . , like a fire bell in the night, awakened and filled me with terror. I considered it at once as the knell of the Union. It is hushed indeed for the moment. But this is a reprieve only, not a final sentence."*
>
> —Thomas Jefferson

1823

At the urging of Secretary of State John Quincy Adams, President James Monroe sets forth what will become known as the Monroe Doctrine.

> *"The American continents, by the free and independent condition which they have assumed and maintain, are henceforth not to be considered as subjects for future colonization by any European powers."*
>
> —James Monroe

1824

Andrew Jackson wins more electoral votes than any other presidential candidate but not a majority, causing the election to be thrown into the House of Representatives. The House chooses John Quincy Adams.

Jackson also had the most popular votes in 1824, but at that time six states had no popular vote for president. Then—as now—the Constitution provided for each state to determine how electors were chosen, and in those six states the legislatures made the decision.

1825

The completion of the 363-mile-long Erie Canal joins the Hudson River and the Great Lakes. The opening of the canal spurs trade between New York City and territory to the west.

> *'Tis not that this union our coffers may fill—*
> *Oh! no—it is something more exquisite still.*
> *'Tis, that genius has triumphed—and science*
> *prevailed.*
>
> —Song sung at the opening of the Erie Canal

1826

Charles Grandison Finney's revival meeting in Utica, New York, gives impetus to the Second Great Awakening, which will bring hundreds of thousands to a renewal of faith.

> *"On my arrival in the United States it was the religious aspect of the country that first struck my eye."*
>
> —Alexis de Tocqueville

1828

Andrew Jackson defeats John Quincy Adams and is elected president. He is the first president from west of the Appalachians.

Jackson suffered considerably from a bullet lodged in his chest. It came from an 1806 duel—over a wager on a horse race—in which his opponent fired first and wounded him. Jackson subsequently shot and killed his opponent. Jackson also had a bullet in his arm, from an 1813 gunfight, that caused him pain from time to time. He had it removed in 1832.

1830

When Senator Robert Hayne of South Carolina argues that a state can nullify a federal law, Daniel Webster of Massachusetts defends the Union in what may be the most famous speech ever given on the Senate floor.

> *"When my eyes shall be turned to behold for the last time the sun in heaven, may I not see him shining on the broken and dishonored fragments of a once glorious Union; on States dissevered, discordant, belligerent; on a land rent with civil feuds, or drenched, it may be, in fraternal blood! Let their last feeble and lingering glance rather behold the gorgeous ensign of the republic, . . . bearing for its motto, . . . Liberty and Union, now and forever, one and inseparable!"*
>
> —Senator Daniel Webster

No one was sure where President Jackson stood on the issue of state sovereignty, but he soon made his position clear with a toast offered at a Washington dinner.

"Our federal Union: It must be preserved."

—PRESIDENT ANDREW JACKSON

"The Union: next to our liberty, the most dear."

—VICE PRESIDENT JOHN C. CALHOUN, from South Carolina, offering a toast after the president

1830

At the urging of President Jackson, Congress passes an act providing for the removal of all Indians to the west side of the Mississippi River. Over the next few decades tens of thousands will be forcibly moved.

THE ROUTE TAKEN BY CHEROKEES FROM GEORGIA, TENNESSEE, ALABAMA, AND NORTH CAROLINA TO OKLAHOMA IS CALLED THE TRAIL OF TEARS. THOUSANDS PERISHED ALONG THE WAY.

1831

William Lloyd Garrison begins publishing his newspaper the *Liberator* in Boston. In it he demands a complete and immediate end to slavery.

"I *am in earnest*—I *will not equivocate*—I *will not excuse*—I *will not retreat a single inch*—AND I WILL BE HEARD."

—WILLIAM LLOYD GARRISON

1832

President Jackson vetoes a bill renewing the charter for the Second Bank of the United States.

PREVIOUS PRESIDENTS HAD VETOED BILLS ON THE GROUNDS THAT THEY WERE UNCONSTITUTIONAL. WITH HIS VETO OF THE BANK BILL, JACKSON CLAIMED THE RIGHT FOR PRESIDENTS TO VETO A BILL FOR ANY REASON. IN HIS VETO MESSAGE HE CONDEMNED THE BANK AS A TOOL OF THE RICH AND POWERFUL.

1832

In a presidential election in which the Second Bank of the United States is the chief issue, President Jackson—with Martin Van Buren as his vice presidential running mate—prevails over his rival, Senator Henry Clay.

1832

President Jackson issues a nullification proclamation to deal with South Carolina's having repudiated federal tariff acts. In the New Year he will resolve the dispute by signing both a force bill, which underscores his ability to compel South Carolina's compliance, and a bill lowering the tariffs to which South Carolinians objected.

1833

Rather than let the charter for the Second Bank of the United States run out (it still has several years to go), President Jackson sets about destroying the Bank. He directs that federal monies be withdrawn.

IN THE COURSE OF BRINGING ABOUT THE END OF THE BANK, JACKSON SHOCKED MEMBERS OF THE SENATE BY CLAIMING TO BE RESPONSIBLE NOT TO THEM, BUT TO THE PEOPLE.

"The president is the direct representative of the American people."

—PRESIDENT ANDREW JACKSON

1834

Calling President Jackson "King Andrew I," opponents of the president join in a coalition that will form a new political entity, the Whig Party.

1836

Determined to assert Mexico's authority over Texas, Gen. Antonio López de Santa Anna and 1,800 troops lay siege to the Alamo and kill the 189 men defending the fort, including Col. William B. Travis, James Bowie, and Davy Crockett. Two months later Gen. Sam Houston, commanding forces of the newly proclaimed Republic of Texas, will defeat Mexican forces at San Jacinto and capture Santa Anna.

"I shall never surrender or retreat."

—WILLIAM B. TRAVIS

THE ALAMO

"Remember the Alamo!"

—Rallying cry for Texas troops at the Battle of San Jacinto

1836

Arkansas enters the Union as the twenty-fifth state.

1836

Martin Van Buren, triumphing over several Whig candidates, is elected president of the United States.

1837

Michigan enters the Union as the twenty-sixth state.

1838

Frederick Douglass escapes from slavery in Maryland and heads north, where he will become an eloquent spokesman in the antislavery cause.

Frederick Douglass

DOUGLASS HONED HIS ELOQUENCE ON A BOOK OF ANCIENT AND MODERN SPEECHES CALLED *THE COLUMBIAN ORATOR*, WHICH HE PURCHASED WHEN HE WAS TWELVE YEARS OLD FOR FIFTY CENTS, A SUBSTANTIAL SUM AT THE TIME, ESPECIALLY FOR A BOY WHO WAS ENSLAVED.

1839

Enslaved Africans take over the Spanish schooner *Amistad*, killing its captain. A case against them will reach the Supreme Court, which will order them freed.

> *"Little did I imagine that I should ever again be required to claim the right of appearing in the capacity of an officer of this Court; yet such has been the dictate of my destiny—and I appear again to plead the cause of justice, and now of liberty and life, in behalf of many of my fellow men."*
>
> —Former president JOHN QUINCY ADAMS, defending the Amistad captives in his seventy-fourth year

1840

William Henry Harrison, hero of Tippecanoe and a Whig, is elected president. He will die one month after his inauguration and be succeeded by his vice president, John Tyler.

> *"Tippecanoe and Tyler too."*
>
> —The Whig presidential campaign slogan

1843

Missionary Marcus Whitman helps lead a train of more than a hundred wagons from Missouri to the Columbia River valley. These pioneers are the first major party to travel the Oregon Trail.

When many of the Indians to whom Marcus and his wife, Narcissa, ministered became sick with measles and died, the Indians blamed the Whitmans. A small group murdered eighteen at the Whitman mission, including Marcus, Narcissa, and two orphans for whom they had been caring.

1844

Samuel F. B. Morse transmits a telegraph message between Washington, D.C., and Baltimore, Maryland. Within two decades it will be possible to send a message across the continent.

> *"What hath God wrought?"*
>
> —Samuel F. B. Morse, in a telegraph message from the U.S. Capitol to Alfred Vail in Baltimore

1844

James K. Polk, a Democrat, defeats Henry Clay, the Whig candidate, for the presidency of the United States.

President James K. Polk

1845

As potato crops begin failing in Ireland, immigrants fleeing famine and poverty come to America. By 1860 nearly two million will have entered the United States, most to live in crowded tenements in coastal cities.

Among those leaving Ireland for America were Edward and Mary O'Neill, whose grandson Eugene became a playwright; John and Thomasina Ford, whose grandson Henry became famous for cars; and Patrick Kennedy and Bridget Murphy, whose great-grandson John became president of the United States.

1845

Florida enters the Union as the twenty-seventh state.

1845

Texas enters the Union as the twenty-eighth state. Because it has been an independent republic, it is annexed by a joint resolution of Congress, which the voters of Texas approve. Mexico considers the annexation an act of war, but many Americans respond with enthusiasm.

> "*Our manifest destiny* [is] *to overspread the continent allotted by Providence for the free development of our yearly multiplying millions.*"
>
> —John O'Sullivan, journal editor, arguing for the annexation of Texas

> "*Ah!* [The American flag's] *broad folds are destined to float yet—and we, haply, shall see them—over many a good square mile which now owns a far different emblem.*"
>
> —Walt Whitman, newspaper editor and poet

1846

President James K. Polk sends troops into disputed territory along the Rio Grande. When Mexican forces conduct a raid into the disputed territory, Polk asks for a declaration of war against Mexico, which Congress provides on May 13.

> "*As war exists, and, notwithstanding all our efforts to avoid it, exists by the act of Mexico herself, we are called upon by every consideration of duty and patriotism, to vindicate with decision, the honor, the right, and the interests of our country.*"
>
> —President James K. Polk

1846

Declaring California independent of Mexico, some thirty Americans raise a flag displaying a star, a stripe, and a bear. Shortly thereafter U.S. naval forces raise the American flag over Monterey and declare California to be part of the United States.

THE LAND KNOWN AS CALIFORNIA WOULD EVENTUALLY FORM THE STATES OF CALIFORNIA, NEVADA, AND UTAH, AS WELL AS PARTS OF ARIZONA, WYOMING, COLORADO, AND NEW MEXICO.

1846

President Polk reaches a compromise with Great Britain that gives the United States sole claim to Oregon Country south of the forty-ninth parallel.

SETTLERS ON THE OREGON TRAIL

OREGON COUNTRY EVENTUALLY FORMED THE STATES OF OREGON, WASHINGTON, AND IDAHO, AS WELL AS PARTS OF WYOMING AND MONTANA.

1846

Pennsylvania congressman David Wilmot proposes a measure that will prohibit slavery in any territory acquired from Mexico. The fury of southerners will grow as antislavery forces introduce the Wilmot Proviso again in 1847 and 1848.

> *"I say, for one, I would rather meet any extremity upon earth than give up one inch of our equality—one inch of what belongs to us as members of this great republic."*
>
> —Senator John C. Calhoun, speaking as "a cotton planter . . . a southern man, and a slaveholder"

1846

Iowa enters the Union as the twenty-ninth state.

1847

American troops under the command of Winfield Scott seize the castle at Chapultepec and capture Mexico City.

THIS AMERICAN VICTORY IS COMMEMORATED IN THE FIRST LINE OF THE MARINE CORPS HYMN, AS IS MARINE BRAVERY IN LEADING A RAID IN TRIPOLI DURING THE FIRST BARBARY WAR.

From the halls of Montezuma
to the shores of Tripoli,
We fight our country's battles
In the air, on land, and sea.

—"Marines' Hymn," as sung today

Zachary Taylor, the man who succeeded James K. Polk as president, fought in the Mexican War, as did Jefferson Davis, who later became the president of the Confederacy. Among the Civil War generals who served in the Mexican War were Ulysses S. Grant, Robert E. Lee, Thomas "Stonewall" Jackson, George B. McClellan, George Pickett, George Meade, and James Longstreet.

1848

The Treaty of Guadalupe Hidalgo ends the Mexican War on American terms: Mexico recognizes American claims to California and New Mexico as well as the Rio Grande boundary with Texas.

Although the Mexican War added more than 525,000 square miles to the United States, it had notable opponents. Abraham Lincoln, a freshman congressman, voted for a resolution declaring the war unnecessary. Henry David Thoreau protested by refusing to pay his poll tax and going to jail.

"I heartily accept the motto,–'That government is best which governs least'; and I should like to see it acted up to more rapidly and systematically. Carried out, it finally amounts to this, which also I believe,–'That government is best which governs not at all.'"

—HENRY DAVID THOREAU

1848

Wisconsin enters the Union as the thirtieth state.

1848

Mormons traveling in more than nine hundred wagons cross from the Missouri River to the valley of the Great Salt Lake, which their leader, Brigham Young, has declared to be the place that they should settle. Over the next twenty years tens of thousands will follow on the Mormon Trail.

"We have suffered and endured such a continuation of persecution and cruel treatment from those who boast of civilization that we now choose to make our home in the desert among savages rather than try to live in the garden of the world surrounded by Christian neighbors."

—JOHN PULSIPHER, who celebrated his twenty-first birthday on the trail

---

IN THE MID-1850S A FEW THOUSAND MORMONS, MOSTLY POOR CONVERTS FROM ENGLAND, TRAVELED THE THIRTEEN-HUNDRED-MILE TRAIL PULLING HANDCARTS. MANY SICKENED AND DIED.

1848

Antislavery activists Lucretia Mott and Elizabeth Cady Stanton hold a convention in Seneca Falls, New York, to discuss the rights of women.

> *"All men and women are created equal."*
>
> —Declaration of Sentiments, issued at Seneca Falls

1848

Zachary Taylor, a Whig, is elected president of the United States. In 1850 he will die in office and be succeeded by Millard Fillmore.

1849

After James Marshall discovers gold at Sutter's Mill, tens of thousands rush to California, many by ship.

1849

Harriet Tubman, born in slavery, escapes to the North and freedom. She will make frequent trips back to the South to help others escape.

1850

With animosity between North and South growing, Senator Henry Clay of Kentucky offers compromise proposals, including the admission of California as a free state and the enactment of a more effective law dealing with fugitive slaves.

SENATOR JOHN C. CALHOUN ARGUED AGAINST CLAY'S COMPROMISE, ON THE GROUNDS THAT IT DID NOT DO JUSTICE TO THE SOUTH, BUT EVEN WHEN OPPOSING THE KENTUCKIAN, CALHOUN—LIKE MANY

OTHERS—COULD NOT RESIST HIS CHARM. "I DON'T LIKE HENRY CLAY," CALHOUN ONCE SAID. "I WOULDN'T SPEAK TO HIM, BUT, BY GOD, I LOVE HIM."

Henry Clay speaking in the Senate

"Mr. President, I wish to speak today, not as a Massachusetts man, nor as a northern man, but as an American. . . . I speak today for the preservation of the Union. Hear me for my cause."

—Senator Daniel Webster, advocating the compromise measures that subsequently passed and became known as the Compromise of 1850

So fallen! So lost! The light withdrawn
Which once he wore!
The glory from his gray hairs gone
Forevermore!

—Poet John Greenleaf Whittier, dismayed that Daniel Webster supported a compromise strengthening fugitive slave laws

1850

California enters the Union as the thirty-first state.

1851–52

Harriet Beecher Stowe publishes *Uncle Tom's Cabin*, a novel depicting the cruelties of slavery.

Harriet Beecher Stowe

> *"So this is the little lady who wrote the book that made this great war."*
>
> —Abraham Lincoln's words upon meeting Mrs. Stowe, according to legend

1852

Franklin Pierce, a Democrat, defeats Whig Winfield Scott for the presidency.

1853

Commodore Matthew Perry sails four warships into Japan's Edo Bay. The next year the Japanese, who have generally kept their country closed to outsiders for more than two centuries, will agree to permit limited trade and to allow whalers and other ships to take on provisions.

In the early 1850s, with the whaling industry at its height, Herman Melville published the novel *Moby-Dick,* a depiction of whaling life that ponders epic questions. *Moby-Dick* is widely held to be a masterpiece today, but during Melville's lifetime the book sold only about three thousand copies.

1853

Sent to Mexico by Secretary of War Jefferson Davis, James Gadsden arranges for the United States to purchase a southwestern strip of land needed for construction of the Southern Pacific Railroad. When the sale is approved, the borders containing the forty-eight lower states become those we are familiar with today.

Davis believed that extending a railway from the South to the Pacific Ocean would be a great advantage to the South should there be war with the North. But a southern transcontinental route was not completed until 1881, sixteen years after the Civil War was over.

1854

The Kansas-Nebraska Act, introduced by Illinois senator Stephen A. Douglas, becomes law, repealing the part of the Missouri Compromise that prohibits slavery north of latitude 36°30' and mandating popular sovereignty—that is, leaving it up to the people to decide whether to permit slavery. Kansas becomes a place of murder and violence as proslavery and antislavery forces struggle to prevail.

SENATOR DOUGLAS WANTED TO ORGANIZE THE GREAT PLAINS SO THAT A RAILROAD ROUTE COULD GO THROUGH THEM. SOUTHERNERS, WHO WANTED THEIR OWN ROUTE, WOULD HAVE OPPOSED SUCH AN ATTEMPT HAD IT NOT BEEN FOR THE FACT THAT THE KANSAS-NEBRASKA ACT OVERTURNED THE MISSOURI COMPROMISE AND THUS LIFTED A PROHIBITION AGAINST SLAVERY.

1856

The Republican Party, a new political party opposed to slavery in the territories, holds a national convention in Philadelphia. Their candidate for president, John C. Frémont, is defeated in the general election by Democrat James Buchanan, who carries most of the South.

1857

The Supreme Court rejects the claim of Dred Scott, a slave, that he should be free because he has resided in territory where Congress has prohibited slavery. As one of the grounds for its decision, the Court declares that Congress has no right to deprive citizens of their property.

IN 1857, SHORTLY AFTER THE *DRED SCOTT* DECISION, IRENE EMERSON, SCOTT'S OWNER, MARRIED A MAN OPPOSED TO SLAVERY. SHE RETURNED SCOTT AND HIS FAMILY TO THEIR PREVIOUS OWNERS, THE BLOW FAMILY, AND THEY GRANTED HIM AND HIS FAMILY THEIR FREEDOM. IN 1858 SCOTT DIED OF TUBERCULOSIS.

Dred Scott

1858

Minnesota enters the Union as the thirty-second state.

1858

Abraham Lincoln and Stephen Douglas, U.S. Senate candidates from Illinois, engage in a series of debates. Lincoln loses the election but gains recognition that will help him become the Republican presidential candidate in 1860.

> "'*A house divided against itself cannot stand.*' I *believe this government cannot endure permanently half slave and half free. I do not expect the Union to be dissolved—I do not expect the house to fall—but I do expect it will cease to be divided. It will become all one thing, or all the other.*"
>
> —Abraham Lincoln, U.S. Senate candidate

1859

Oregon enters the Union as the thirty-third state. There are now eighteen free and fifteen slave states.

1859

John Brown, an abolitionist hoping to inspire a slave uprising, seizes the federal arsenal at Harpers Ferry. He is convicted of treason and hanged.

> *"I, John Brown, am now quite certain that the crimes of this guilty land will never be purged away but with blood."*
>
> —John Brown, on the day of his execution

> *"The new saint . . . will make the gallows glorious like the cross."*
>
> —Ralph Waldo Emerson, speaking of John Brown

There were four million enslaved people in the South, and uprisings had occurred, most notably in South Carolina and Virginia. Since worry about slave rebellion was never far from the minds of white southerners, they were particularly bitter about the sympathy of some northerners for John Brown.

1860

Abraham Lincoln, carrying every free state, is elected president of the United States.

Lincoln in 1860

1860

South Carolina secedes from the Union. In the next five months ten other states will also become part of the Confederacy. Mississippi's Jefferson Davis will become president of the Confederate States.

1861

Kansas is the thirty-fourth state to enter the Union.

1861

President Lincoln is inaugurated.

> "*We must not be enemies. Though passion may have strained, it must not break our bonds of affection. The mystic chords of memory, stretching from every battle-field, and patriot grave, to every living heart and hearthstone, all over this broad land, will yet swell the chorus of the Union, when again touched, as surely they will be, by the better angels of our nature.*"
>
> —President Abraham Lincoln

1861

Confederate forces fire on Fort Sumter, a federal fort in Charleston Harbor, and the Civil War begins.

> *"The intelligence that Fort Sumter surrendered to the Confederate forces . . . sent a thrill of joy to the heart of every true friend of the South. The face of every Southern man was brighter, his step lighter, and his bearing prouder, than it had been before."*
>
> —*Montgomery Advertiser*

SHORTLY AFTER FORT SUMTER FELL, ROBERT E. LEE WAS OFFERED COMMAND OF THE UNION ARMY, BUT WHEN HIS NATIVE VIRGINIA SECEDED, HE DECIDED INSTEAD TO COMMAND THE ARMY OF VIRGINIA. "I CANNOT RAISE MY HAND AGAINST MY BIRTHPLACE, MY HOME, MY CHILDREN," HE WROTE.

1861

Union and Confederate troops meet at Bull Run, a stream near Manassas Junction in Virginia. The Northern line breaks, and Union soldiers flee, many back to nearby Washington, D.C.

A SOUTH CAROLINA GENERAL, OBSERVING A CONFEDERATE COMMANDER WHO WAS UNWAVERING AS HE HELD THE CENTER OF THE SOUTHERN LINE, SHOUTED, "THERE STANDS JACKSON LIKE A STONE WALL." AND THUS IT WAS THAT THOMAS JACKSON WAS EVER AFTER KNOWN AS STONEWALL.

1861

Julia Ward Howe visits a Union army camp and composes the words to the Civil War's best-known song.

> *He has sounded forth the trumpet that shall never*
> *call retreat:*
> *He is sifting out the hearts of men before* His
> *judgment seat:*
> *Oh, be swift, my soul, to answer* Him! *be jubilant*
> *my feet!*
> Our God *is marching on!*
>
> —JULIA WARD HOWE, published version of "Battle Hymn of the Republic"

1862

Two ironclad ships, the Union *Monitor* and the Confederate *Virginia* (originally named the *Merrimack*), fight in waters off Norfolk, Virginia. Although the battle is a draw, both ships withstand so much firepower that it is clear the day of the wooden navy is over.

1862

With the South having seceded, Congress passes the Homestead Act, which was opposed by Southerners worried that homesteaders would oppose slavery in the territories. The act provides 160 acres of land to settlers who live on it for five years and pay a nominal fee.

THE HOMESTEAD ACT DREW PEOPLE WEST INTO THE NEXT CENTURY, AND SOME OF THOSE WHO FILED FOR LAND WERE WOMEN. AS LONG AS THEY WERE THE HEAD OF THEIR FAMILY, THEY WERE ELIGIBLE FOR HOMESTEADS.

"I have a grove of twelve swamp pines on my place, and I am going to build my house there."

—Elinore Pruitt Stewart, a widow who filed for a homestead in Wyoming in 1909

1862

President Abraham Lincoln signs the Morrill Land-Grant College Act, giving every state remaining in the Union tens of thousands of acres of land to sell. States are to use the proceeds to establish colleges. After the war land grants will be extended to southern states.

1862

At the Second Battle of Bull Run, Confederate forces again defeat the Union.

"The ground . . . was a thinly wooded slope—and among the trees on the leaves and grass were laid the wounded, who were pouring in by scores of wagon loads."

—Clara Barton, who helped the wounded at Bull Run and later founded the American Red Cross

1862

Following the Confederate victory at Bull Run, Gen. Robert E. Lee invades Maryland, but his offensive into the North is stopped at Antietam, where the single bloodiest day of fighting in the Civil War occurs. Six thousand are killed, and sixteen thousand are wounded.

In the days leading up to the Battle of Antietam, two Union soldiers found a copy of Lee's orders, dropped by a careless Confederate officer. The orders showed that Lee had divided his forces, but by moving too slowly, the Union commander, Gen. George B. McClellan, lost the advantage this intelligence should have provided.

1863

President Lincoln issues the Emancipation Proclamation.

"On the first day of January, in the year of our Lord one thousand eight hundred and sixty-three, all persons held as slaves within any state or designated part of a state, the people whereof shall then be in rebellion against the United States, shall be then, thenceforward, and forever, free."

—President Abraham Lincoln

"The first step on the part of the nation in its departure from the thraldom of ages."

—Frederick Douglass, describing the Emancipation Proclamation

The Emancipation Proclamation also provided for receiving Southern freedmen and Northern blacks into the Union army and navy. By the end of the Civil War, almost two hundred thousand had served.

Ulysses S. Grant

Robert E. Lee

1863

West Virginia is the thirty-fifth state to enter the Union.

1863

General Lee once again moves north, this time into Pennsylvania, where 75,000 Confederate troops meet 85,000 Union troops at Gettysburg. In the bloodiest battle of the war, the North is victorious.

The Battle of Gettysburg

On the third day of battle, Lee ordered Gen. James Longstreet to charge the center of the Union line with Gen. George Pickett's division and two others. Half of the 14,000 Confederate soldiers who charged forward were killed, wounded, or captured. General Lee wrote to Jefferson Davis offering to resign, but his offer was rejected.

1863

When draft officers in New York City begin drawing the names of those to be called in the Union's first draft, riots break out that leave more than a hundred dead.

Draftees could avoid service by paying a fee of $300. Of the 207,000 who were drafted, 87,000 chose to pay. Another 74,000 chose to hire a substitute. During the remaining years of the war, nearly 800,000 men enlisted or reenlisted, and they often earned a bounty for doing so.

1863

Four and a half months after the Battle of Gettysburg, President Lincoln travels to the battlefield and gives an address that lasts about three minutes.

> *"Fourscore and seven years ago our fathers brought forth on this continent, a new nation, conceived in liberty, and dedicated to the proposition that all men are created equal. Now we are engaged in a great*

civil war, testing whether that nation, or any nation so conceived and so dedicated, can long endure."

—PRESIDENT ABRAHAM LINCOLN, from the Gettysburg Address

1864

Lincoln gives command of the Union army to Ulysses S. Grant, who has been commanding Union forces in the western theater.

PRESIDENT ABRAHAM LINCOLN AND HIS SON TAD

IN THE MONTHS FOLLOWING GRANT'S APPOINTMENT, BOTH SIDES SUSTAINED TERRIBLE LOSSES: THE NUMBER OF UNION DEAD AND WOUNDED WAS 65,000. CONFEDERATE LOSSES WERE 35,000, A SMALLER NUMBER BUT EQUALLY DEVASTATING FOR THE SOUTH'S SMALLER ARMY.

> *"General Grant is reported to have said, I am going through on this line if it takes all summer. . . . I say we are going through on this line if it takes three years more."*
>
> —President Abraham Lincoln

1864

Under orders from General Grant, William Tecumseh Sherman captures Atlanta. He will set fire to the city and march with his army to Savannah, devastating the countryside along the way.

> *"Since Atlanta I have felt as if all were dead within me, forever."*
>
> —Mary Chesnut, a South Carolinian

1864

Nevada is the thirty-sixth state to enter the Union.

1864

Two months after the burning of Atlanta, Abraham Lincoln is elected to a second term.

> *"With malice toward none, with charity for all, with firmness in the right as God gives us to see the right, let us strive on to finish the work we are in, to bind up the nation's wounds, to care for him who shall have borne the battle and for his widow and his orphan, to do all which may achieve and cherish a just and lasting peace among ourselves and with all nations."*
>
> —President Abraham Lincoln, in his second inaugural address

1865

After a nine-and-a-half-month siege General Grant launches an all-out attack on Petersburg, a town near Richmond, the Confederate capital. As Union forces march into Petersburg, the Confederate government flees from Richmond, which is soon after occupied by Union forces.

ABRAHAM LINCOLN, ACCOMPANIED BY HIS SON TAD, VISITED RICHMOND SHORTLY AFTER THE CITY WAS CAPTURED. AS HE WALKED THROUGH THE STREETS, FREEDMEN AND FREEDWOMEN MOBBED HIM. "I KNOW I AM FREE," SAID ONE, "FOR I HAVE SEEN FATHER ABRAHAM AND FELT HIM."

1865

Gen. Robert E. Lee surrenders to Gen. Ulysses S. Grant at Appomattox Court House, a village in Virginia.

> *"I felt like anything rather than rejoicing at the downfall of a foe who had fought so long and valiantly, and had suffered so much for a cause, though that cause was, I believe, one of the worst for which a people ever fought."*
>
> —Gen. Ulysses S. Grant

A FEW DAYS LATER, WHEN CONFEDERATE TROOPS APPROACHED TO SURRENDER, UNION GENERAL JOSHUA CHAMBERLAIN OF MAINE, A HERO OF GETTYSBURG, ORDERED HIS MEN INTO LINE. AS CONFEDERATE TROOPS PASSED BEFORE THEM, THE SOLDIERS OF THE UNION SNAPPED TO A SALUTE OF HONOR.

1865

Five days after Lee's surrender, Abraham Lincoln is fatally shot by an assassin while attending a play at Ford's Theatre. He will die the next day.

O Captain! my Captain! our fearful trip is done;
The ship has weather'd every rack, the prize we
sought is won;
The port is near, the bells I hear, the people all
exulting,
While follow eyes the steady keel, the vessel grim
and daring:
But O heart! heart! heart!
O the bleeding drops of red,
Where on the deck my Captain lies,
Fallen cold and dead.

—Walt Whitman

President Abraham Lincoln

FOUR

A NATION ONCE MORE

1865

After Abraham Lincoln's assassination Andrew Johnson of Tennessee becomes president. His conciliatory policy toward the South angers those known as Radical Republicans, who favor a tougher approach and are determined to insure the rights of former slaves.

> *"If we have not yet been sufficiently scourged for our national sin to teach us to do justice to all God's creatures, without distinction of race or color, we must expect the still more heavy vengeance of an offended Father."*
>
> —Thaddeus Stevens, leader of the Radical Republicans, in the House of Representatives, December 1865

SEVENTY-THREE-YEAR-OLD STEVENS WAS SO ILL WHEN HE ADDRESSED THE HOUSE OF REPRESENTATIVES IN DECEMBER 1865 THAT HE COULD NOT WALK MORE THAN A FEW STEPS AT A TIME. HE HAD TWO MEN CARRY HIM EVERYWHERE, INCLUDING INTO THE HOUSE CHAMBER, IN A SPECIAL CHAIR.

1865

The Thirteenth Amendment to the Constitution, which abolishes slavery, is ratified by three fourths of the reunited states.

"Neither slavery nor involuntary servitude, except as a punishment for crime whereof the party shall have been duly convicted, shall exist within the United States, or any place subject to their jurisdiction."

—The Thirteenth Amendment

1866

Spurred on by the enactment in former Confederate states of Black Codes limiting the rights of African Americans, Congress passes a civil rights act and a bill extending the Freedmen's Bureau. When President Andrew Johnson vetoes these bills, the Congress overrides his vetoes, and the bills become law.

WHEN CONGRESS PASSED THE CIVIL RIGHTS ACT IN APRIL 1866, IT WAS THE FIRST TIME THAT A MAJOR PIECE OF LEGISLATION HAD BECOME LAW OVER A PRESIDENT'S VETO.

1866

Congress passes the Fourteenth Amendment to the Constitution, which says that all persons born or naturalized in the United States are citizens and gives federal protection to individual rights. Ten of the eleven former Confederate states, Tennessee being the exception, will reject the amendment.

"No state shall make or enforce any law which shall abridge the privileges or immunities of citizens of the United States; nor shall any state deprive any person of life, liberty, or property, without due process of law;

nor deny to any person within its jurisdiction the equal protection of the laws."

—The Fourteenth Amendment

THE FOURTEENTH AMENDMENT ALSO SAID THAT THE NUMBER OF REPRESENTATIVES APPORTIONED TO A STATE WOULD BE BASED UPON THE NUMBER OF MALE CITIZENS ALLOWED TO VOTE IN THAT STATE, THUS INTRODUCING THE WORD *MALE* INTO THE CONSTITUTION FOR THE FIRST TIME. LEADERS OF THE WOMEN'S MOVEMENT WERE OUTRAGED TO SEE THEIR DISFRANCHISEMENT INSTITUTIONALIZED IN THE COUNTRY'S FOUNDING DOCUMENT.

"The introduction of the word male *. . . is a gross affront to women everywhere."*

—Resolutions of the Equal Rights Convention in Syracuse, New York

"When they asked us to be silent on our question during the war, and labor for the emancipation of the slave, we did so. . . . I was convinced, at the time, that it was the true policy. I am now equally sure that it was a blunder."

—ELIZABETH CADY STANTON, women's rights leader

1867

Nebraska joins the Union as the thirty-seventh state.

1867

Congress passes the Reconstruction Act over President Andrew Johnson's veto. Former Confederate states (except Tennessee) are put under military rule and are required to provide for universal manhood suffrage and to ratify the Fourteenth Amendment. Congress will pass several more Reconstruction Acts after President Johnson vetoes them.

IN A BILL THAT DID NOT PASS, THADDEUS STEVENS PROPOSED THAT THE FEDERAL GOVERNMENT SEIZE CONFEDERATE LANDS AND REDISTRIBUTE THEM TO FORMER SLAVES IN FORTY-ACRE PARCELS.

1867

Secretary of State William Seward agrees to buy Alaska from Russia. Although controversial, the $7 million purchase is approved by the Senate.

1868

When President Johnson fires his secretary of war, thus appearing to violate the Tenure of Office Act, passed by a Republican Congress, the House of Representatives votes to impeach him. The Senate falls one vote short of the necessary two-thirds majority needed to convict him and remove him from office.

> "*I shall ever thank God that in that terrible hour of trial . . . I had the courage to be true to my oath and my conscience.*"
>
> —Republican senator JAMES GRIMES of Iowa, who, although a foe of the president, voted to acquit him

President Johnson receiving impeachment summons

With fifty-four senators, nineteen votes of "not guilty" acquitted the president. All twelve Democratic senators voted "not guilty," as did seven Republicans.

1868

As southern states begin ratifying the Fourteenth Amendment, it achieves the support of three fourths of the states and becomes part of the Constitution.

1868

Thaddeus Stevens dies at age seventy-six.

> *"I have chosen this that I might illustrate in my death the principles which I advocated through a long life, equality of man before his creator."*
>
> —Thaddeus Stevens's epitaph, explaining why he chose to be buried in a racially integrated cemetery

1868

Ulysses S. Grant is elected president on the Republican ticket.

In the 1868 election for president, African-American votes counted in sixteen of the thirty-seven states, eight of them in the former Confederacy and eight in the twenty-six remaining states.

1869

To secure the vote for African-American men in the North as well as the South, Congress passes and sends to the states the Fifteenth Amendment, which will be ratified the following year.

> *"The right of citizens of the United States to vote shall not be denied or abridged by the United States or by any state on account of race, color, or previous condition of servitude."*
>
> —The Fifteenth Amendment

Elizabeth Cady Stanton and Susan B. Anthony

Elizabeth Cady Stanton and her colleague Susan B. Anthony were dismayed that the Fifteenth Amendment did not forbid denial of the right to vote on account of sex. Believing it was time for a new organization composed solely of women and focusing on rights for women, they founded the National Woman Suffrage Association. Thinking this too radical a move, other suffragists started a competing organization.

One of the bridges built for the Union Pacific railway

1869

The Union Pacific railway meets the Central Pacific railway at Promontory Summit in Utah, creating the first transcontinental railroad. Following this accomplishment, the miles of rail line in the United States will increase dramatically, reaching 164,000 by 1890.

"Sir: We have the honor to report that the last rail is laid, the last spike is driven, the Pacific Railroad is finished."

—LELAND STANFORD, Central Pacific president, and Thomas Durant, head of Union Pacific, to U.S. president Ulysses S. Grant

---

ONE OF THE CENTURY'S GREATEST ACHIEVEMENTS, THE RAILROAD ALSO GAVE RISE TO THE ERA'S BIGGEST SCANDAL. THE CRÉDIT MOBILIER, A COMPANY CREATED TO BUILD THE UNION PACIFIC, PAID HUGE DIVIDENDS TO SHAREHOLDERS, INCLUDING CONGRESSMEN, AT THE SAME TIME THAT THE RAILROAD ITSELF WAS UNABLE TO PAY WORKMEN OR ITS DEBTS. "THE KING OF FRAUDS," ONE NEWSPAPER CALLED IT.

1869

Wyoming Territory, recognizing women's right to vote, grants full female suffrage. When Wyoming becomes a state in 1890, it will be the only state in which women have full voting rights.

"Wyoming is the first place on God's green earth which could consistently claim to be the land of the free!"

—SUSAN B. ANTHONY, women's rights leader

IT WAS 1917 BEFORE ANY STATE EAST OF THE MISSISSIPPI GRANTED WOMEN FULL VOTING RIGHTS. IN THE MEANTIME, WOMEN WERE FULLY ENFRANCHISED IN MANY PLACES IN THE WEST: WYOMING, COLORADO,

Utah, Idaho, Washington, California, Oregon, Kansas, Arizona, Montana, Nevada, and Alaska territory.

1870

Hiram Revels of Mississippi, a minister of the African Methodist Episcopal Church, becomes the first African American to serve in the United States Senate. He fills the remaining unexpired term of Jefferson Davis, who was president of the Confederacy.

Hiram Revels

1871

In response to a campaign of terror by the Ku Klux Klan against black citizens and white Republicans in the South, Congress passes a law making the violation of civil or political rights a federal crime.

1872

President Ulysses S. Grant signs a bill setting aside 2.2 million acres as the first national park: Yellowstone.

Upper Yellowstone Falls

Fur trappers who had reported on the geysers and boiling pools of Yellowstone were thought to be telling tall tales. An 1870 expedition led by Henry Washburn, surveyor general of Montana Territory, and an 1871 exploration led by geologist Ferdinand Hayden confirmed what the trappers had said and led to legislation creating the park.

1872

Taking a new approach, suffragists argue that since the Fourteenth Amendment makes women citizens, they ought to be able to vote. When Susan B. Anthony casts a ballot in New York, however, she is arrested for voting illegally.

1875

Congress passes a civil rights act guaranteeing all citizens full and equal access to public facilities.

> *"All persons within the jurisdiction of the United States shall be entitled to the full and equal enjoyment of the accommodations, advantages, facilities, and privileges of inns, public conveyances on land or water, theaters, and other places of public amusement."*
>
> —The Civil Rights Act of 1875

1875

Scottish immigrant Andrew Carnegie opens his first steel plant and fills an order for steel rails for the Pennsylvania Railroad. By the turn of the century, he will be one of the richest men in the world—and begin to give his money away.

> *"This, then, is held to be the duty of the man of wealth: . . . to consider all surplus revenues which come to him simply as trust funds, which he is . . . strictly bound as a matter of duty to administer in the manner which, in his judgment, is best calculated to produce the most beneficial results for the community."*
>
> —Andrew Carnegie

1876

Alexander Graham Bell, a Scottish immigrant and teacher of the deaf, succeeds in transmitting the human voice over a wire.

"I then shouted into [the transmitting instrument] the following sentence: 'Mr. Watson—come here—I want to see you.' To my delight he came and declared that he had heard and understood what I said."

—Alexander Graham Bell

Alexander Graham Bell with early telephone

1876

After scandals during the Grant administration—Crédit Mobilier, the Whiskey Ring, bribery involving Indian trading posts—the two parties nominate the most scandal-free candidates they can find: Samuel Tilden, the scourge of the Tweed Ring, for the Democrats; and Rutherford B. Hayes for the Republicans.

Tilden won the popular vote, but with many electoral votes in dispute, he was one short of a victory in the Electoral College. A

COMMISSION APPOINTED BY CONGRESS TO SETTLE THE ELECTION HAD A MAJORITY OF REPUBLICAN MEMBERS, AND BY AWARDING DISPUTED VOTES TO HAYES, THEY MADE HIM PRESIDENT.

MANY SOUTHERN DEMOCRATS WHO MIGHT HAVE DISPUTED THE OUTCOME WENT ALONG WITH IT, BELIEVING THAT HAYES WOULD END RECONSTRUCTION. SHORTLY AFTER BEING SWORN IN AS PRESIDENT, HE BEGAN WITHDRAWING THE LAST FEDERAL TROOPS FROM THE SOUTH. RECONSTRUCTION WAS OVER.

1876

When thousands of miners rush into the Black Hills, where gold has been discovered, the Sioux resist. Lt. Col. George Armstrong Custer, leading a detachment of the Seventh Cavalry, meets Sioux and Cheyenne warriors in the valley of the Little Bighorn River and is killed, as are all his men.

CRAZY HORSE, A SIOUX LEADER AT LITTLE BIGHORN, SURRENDERED THE NEXT SPRING BECAUSE HIS PEOPLE WERE STARVING. HE WAS KILLED BY AN ARMY PRIVATE DURING AN ATTEMPT TO JAIL HIM. SITTING BULL, WHO HAD INSPIRED THE LITTLE BIGHORN WARRIORS, LED HIS PEOPLE TO CANADA BUT WAS FORCED TO RETURN WHEN THEY WERE STARVING. HE WAS KILLED IN 1890 BY SIOUX POLICEMEN TRYING TO ARREST HIM.

FOLLOWING SITTING BULL'S DEATH MANY SIOUX, UNDER ARMY ORDERS, ENCAMPED AT WOUNDED KNEE CREEK. AS U.S. CAVALRY TRIED TO DISARM THE INDIANS, A GUN WENT OFF, THE CAVALRY FIRED, AND AT LEAST 150 SIOUX WERE KILLED, INCLUDING WOMEN AND CHILDREN.

SITTING BULL

1876

Colorado joins the Union as the thirty-eighth state.

1877

As whites crowd onto Nez Percé lands, the U.S. government orders Chief Joseph and his people onto a reservation. When some Nez Percé respond by attacking and murdering whites, Chief Joseph, knowing the army will soon pursue his people, leads them in flight to Canada. They surrender after a journey of more than a thousand miles.

> *"It is cold and we have no blankets. . . . The little children are freezing to death. . . . Hear me, my chiefs;*

I am tired; my heart is sick and sad. From where the sun now stands, I will fight no more forever."

—CHIEF JOSEPH

1879

Thomas Edison creates the first practical incandescent lightbulb.

"Genius is 1 percent inspiration and 99 percent perspiration."

—THOMAS EDISON, who held more than a thousand U.S. patents on his inventions

THOMAS EDISON

1880

James A. Garfield, a Republican, is elected president of the United States. Less than four months after he is sworn in, he will be shot by Charles J. Guiteau, a crazed office seeker. He will die two months later, and Chester A. Arthur will become president.

Presidents were commonly besieged by people wanting jobs, since after an election virtually every position in the federal government was up for grabs. Garfield's assassination created a public outcry for a different approach and resulted in the Pendleton Act, which created a merit system for federal jobs. Eventually all except a few thousand federal jobs fell into this category.

Booker T. Washington

W. E. B. Du Bois

1881

The Tuskegee Normal and Industrial Institute, which will become Tuskegee Institute, then Tuskegee University, opens as a school for African Americans. The school's head, Booker T. Washington, emphasizes vocational education.

As Reconstruction faded into memory and a segregated society emerged, Washington

URGED AFRICAN AMERICANS TO WORK TO IMPROVE THEIR ECONOMIC STATUS RATHER THAN TO SEEK POLITICAL EQUALITY. W. E. B. DU BOIS, AN INTELLECTUAL AND ACTIVIST, DISAGREED SHARPLY, ARGUING FOR POLITICAL ACTION TO SECURE POLITICAL RIGHTS.

1882

John D. Rockefeller, in control of most of America's refineries and pipelines, creates the Standard Oil Trust to coordinate his holdings and monopolize the industry. The creator of the century's largest business empire, he will become an object of scathing attacks by reformers, and a philanthropist of hitherto-unknown scale.

> "*I believe it is my duty to make money and still more money and to use the money I make for the good of my fellow man according to the dictates of my conscience.*"
>
> —JOHN D. ROCKEFELLER

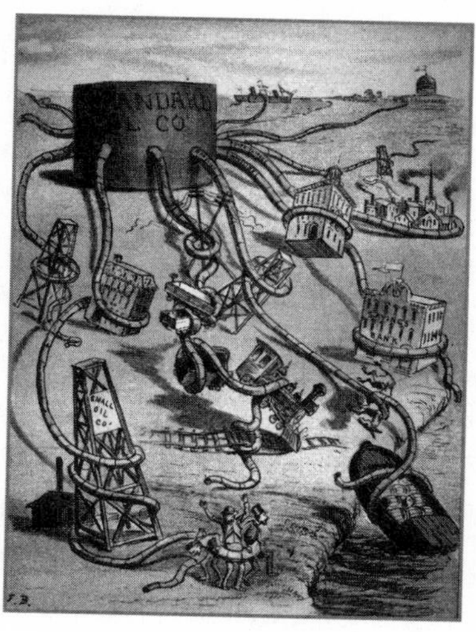

A CARTOONIST'S VIEW OF THE STANDARD OIL MONOPOLY

1882

Congress passes the Chinese Exclusion Act, banning Chinese laborers from immigrating to America. The act will remain in effect until 1943.

1883

The Supreme Court declares the Civil Rights Act of 1875, which outlawed discrimination in public facilities, unconstitutional.

> "*I am of opinion that such discrimination is a badge of servitude, the imposition of which Congress may prevent under its power.*"
>
> —Justice John Harlan, dissenting

The Court's decision encouraged southern states to enact Jim Crow laws, which legalized segregation and prevented African Americans from voting. These laws defined life in the South for decades to come.

1884

With the help of Mugwumps—Republicans who refuse to support James G. Blaine, the nominee of their own party—Democrats succeed in electing Grover Cleveland, the first president of their party since before the Civil War.

Cleveland was the only president elected between the Civil War and the end of the century who did not serve in the war. He is also the only president to serve two non-consecutive terms and the only president to hold a White House wedding for himself.

1886

When a strike at McCormick Reaper Works in Chicago turns into a riot, police kill two strikers. A protest rally organized by anarchists near Haymarket Square becomes even more violent: A bomb is thrown, and eight policemen are killed.

> *"The time will come when our silence will be more powerful than the voices you strangle today."*
>
> —AUGUST SPIES, anarchist labor leader, before his execution

IN THESE TUMULTUOUS DECADES IT WAS NOT UNCOMMON FOR STRIKES TO LEAD TO VIOLENCE. IN 1892 A GUN BATTLE BETWEEN STEELWORKERS AND PINKERTON GUARDS KILLED SIXTEEN AT ANDREW CARNEGIE'S PLANT IN HOMESTEAD, PENNSYLVANIA. IN 1894, IN THE PULLMAN STRIKE IN CHICAGO, TWELVE STRIKERS WERE KILLED AND HUNDREDS WERE ARRESTED.

1880s

Russian Jews, fleeing persecution, begin to immigrate in large numbers, as do others from eastern and southern Europe. From 1880 to the mid-1920s some twenty-three million immigrants will come to the United States.

> *"Here was the gate of the great world opening up before me, with its long open roads radiating in all directions."*
>
> —MARCUS RAVAGE, a sixteen-year-old, getting on the ship that started his journey to America

"The gold you will find in America will not be in the streets. . . . It will be in the dreams you will realize—in the golden dreams of the future."

—An Italian grandmother, bidding farewell to her grandson Leonard Covello, who is leaving for America

Statue of Liberty

1886

The Statue of Liberty is dedicated.

"Give me your tired, your poor,
Your huddled masses yearning to breathe free,
The wretched refuse of your teeming shore.
Send these, the homeless, tempest-tost to me,
I lift my lamp beside the golden door!"

—Emma Lazarus, "The New Colossus," inscribed on a brass plate attached to the pedestal of the Statue of Liberty in 1903

1886

Samuel Gompers is elected president of the American Federation of Labor. Stressing practical goals, he focuses on improving the economic status of skilled workers.

WITH THE EXCEPTION OF ONE YEAR, GOMPERS WAS PRESIDENT OF THE AFL FOR THE NEXT THIRTY-EIGHT YEARS. HE SERVED UNTIL HIS DEATH IN 1924.

1887

The Dawes Act converts tribal lands to individual ownership. The intent is to encourage Indian assimilation. The result is a substantial reduction in lands owned by Native Americans.

1888

Benjamin Harrison, a Republican, is elected president of the United States.

1889

North and South Dakota join the Union as the thirty-ninth and fortieth states.

1889

Montana joins the Union as the forty-first state.

1889

Washington joins the Union as the forty-second state.

1890

Idaho joins the Union as the forty-third state.

1890

Wyoming joins the Union as the forty-fourth state.

1890

Jacob Riis publishes *How the Other Half Lives*, a book showing the dark, overcrowded, unsanitary conditions in the New York tenements in which many new immigrants live. His book will help spur reform.

> *"An epidemic . . . is excessively fatal among the children of the poor, by reason of the practical impossibility of isolating the patient in a tenement. . . .* [Measles] *ravaged three crowded blocks in Elizabeth Street on the heels of the grippe last winter, and, when it had spent its fury, the death-maps in the Bureau of Vital Statistics looked as if a black hand had been laid across those blocks."*
>
> —Jacob Riis

By the end of the century, there were more than a hundred settlement houses, which were community centers aimed at helping the poor. Among the best known: Jane Addams's Hull House in Chicago, Robert Woods's South End House in Boston, and Lillian Wald's Henry Street Settlement in New York City.

1892

Ellis Island opens in New York harbor. Over the next six decades more than twelve million people will enter America through this gateway.

A FAMILY, RECENTLY ARRIVED AT ELLIS ISLAND, VIEWING THE STATUE OF LIBERTY

FOUR OUT OF TEN AMERICANS SAY THEY HAVE A FOREBEAR WHO ENTERED THE UNITED STATES THROUGH ELLIS ISLAND.

1892

Mobs destroy the offices of the *Memphis Free Speech*, a newspaper in which Ida B. Wells has reported on the lynchings of African Americans.

EVERY YEAR FOR DECADES DOZENS OF AFRICAN AMERICANS WERE LYNCHED. THE YEAR 1892 WAS PARTICULARLY VIOLENT, WITH MORE THAN 160 AFRICAN AMERICANS BEING MURDERED THIS WAY.

1892

The superintendent of the census reports that, according to the census of 1890, there is no longer a frontier in the United States—no longer a line where settled area ends and unsettled area begins.

THE CENSUS REPORT INSPIRED HISTORIAN FREDERICK JACKSON TURNER TO REFLECT ON THE MEANING OF THE FRONTIER FOR AMERICAN LIFE. HE TOLD AN AUDIENCE IN CHICAGO IN 1893 THAT THE FRONTIER HAD ENCOURAGED INDIVIDUALISM, FOSTERED DEMOCRACY, AND GIVEN RISE TO "THAT BUOYANCY AND EXUBERANCE WHICH COMES WITH FREEDOM."

1893

In Chicago the World's Columbian Exposition honors the four hundredth anniversary of Columbus's voyage with a dazzling White City built on the shore of Lake Michigan. Millions will attend and marvel at the display of America's industrial and artistic talent.

> *"Make no little plans; they have no magic to stir men's blood."*
>
> —DANIEL BURNHAM, architect and chief builder of the White City

Chicago world exposition

Organizers of the Chicago exposition wanted their fair to outshine one put on in Paris in 1889. The Chicago exposition did draw more visitors on a single day (713,646), and while it did not leave a memorial like the Eiffel Tower, which had been the centerpiece in Paris, it did introduce the world to a large and lovely wheel, the invention of a Mr. Ferris.

1896

Utah joins the Union as the forty-fifth state.

1896

In *Plessy v. Ferguson* the Supreme Court upholds a Louisiana law requiring racial segregation in railroad carriages, saying that "equal but separate" accommodations are legal.

> "*In view of the Constitution, in the eye of the law, there is in this country no superior, dominant, ruling class of citizens. There is no caste here. Our Constitution is color-blind, and neither knows nor tolerates classes among citizens. In respect of civil rights, all citizens are equal before the law.*"
>
> —Justice John Harlan, dissenting

1896

William Jennings Bryan, a former Nebraska congressman, delivers a speech to the Democratic convention in which he proclaims, "You shall not crucify mankind upon a cross of gold." It is a powerful appeal to those who believe that basing the money supply on gold alone (and thus restricting it) helps the wealthy but harms the debt-ridden, particularly farmers.

> "*You come to us and tell us that the great cities are in favor of the gold standard; we reply that the great cities rest upon our broad and fertile prairies. Burn down your cities and leave our farms, and your cities will spring up again as if by magic; but destroy our farms and the grass will grow in the streets of every city in the country.*"
>
> —William Jennings Bryan

WILLIAM JENNINGS BRYAN

AFTER HIS SPEECH, THE DEMOCRATS NOMINATED BRYAN AS THEIR PRESIDENTIAL CANDIDATE. THEY CHOSE HIM TWICE MORE, IN 1900 AND 1908. HE NEVER BECAME PRESIDENT, BUT HE DID BECOME SECRETARY OF STATE IN WOODROW WILSON'S CABINET.

1896

William McKinley is elected president on a party platform demanding independence for Cuba from Spain.

"We want no wars of conquest; we must avoid the temptation of territorial aggression. War should

never be entered upon until every agency of peace has failed; peace is preferable to war in almost every contingency."

—President William McKinley

1898

The USS *Maine* explodes in Havana Harbor, killing some 260 Americans. With the battle cry "Remember the *Maine*" echoing across the country, President McKinley delivers a war message to Congress, which two weeks later declares war on Spain.

In 1976 a group of experts led by Adm. Hyman G. Rickover concluded that the *Maine* likely blew up by accident.

1898

Commodore George Dewey moves against the Spanish base at Manila Bay in the Philippines with four cruisers and two gunboats, destroying the Spanish fleet. When additional U.S. troops arrive, they will capture Manila.

"You may fire when ready, Gridley."

—Commodore Dewey, directing the attack on the Spanish fleet

1898

Under the leadership of Theodore Roosevelt, the Rough Riders, a volunteer regiment, fight at the Battle of San Juan Hill in Cuba. Roosevelt becomes a popular hero.

Theodore Roosevelt and the Rough Riders

Fighting alongside Roosevelt and his Rough Riders were black troops known as Buffalo Soldiers. Six African Americans were awarded Congressional Medals of Honor for their service in the Spanish-American war, including George Wanton, the first African American to receive the medal.

1898

Congress votes to annex Hawaii. It has been five years since American sugar planters overthrew Queen Liliuokalani. In two more years Hawaii will become a U.S. territory.

1898

The treaty ending the Spanish-American War liberates Cuba and puts Puerto Rico, Guam, and the Philippines into American hands.

> *"It has been a splendid little war, begun with the highest motives, carried on with magnificent intelligence and spirit, favored by that fortune which loves the brave."*
>
> —John Hay, to Theodore Roosevelt

One reason the United States prevailed in the Spanish-American War was its navy, and it had a strong navy because of Alfred Thayer Mahan, who in 1890 had published *The Influence of Sea Power upon History, 1660–1783*. Mahan argued that naval power was crucial to a nation's success, and he convinced influential leaders of his belief.

1899

Fighting breaks out between U.S. occupation forces and Filipinos. It will take the United States $160 million and more than three years to put down the revolt.

1900

William McKinley is reelected president. His vice president is Theodore Roosevelt.

William McKinley and Theodore Roosevelet

1900

In experiments led by army doctor Walter Reed, army volunteers and recent Spanish immigrants to Cuba establish that yellow fever is carried by mosquitoes. They demonstrate this by letting themselves be bitten by insects that have first fed on yellow-fever victims.

Several died in the yellow-fever experiments, including Dr. Jesse Lazear, who led early attempts to show that mosquitoes transmitted the disease, and Clara Louise Maass, a nurse on contract with the U.S. Army.

1900

The population of the United States is 76,000,000, according to the United States census.

In 1900 the North American Indian population probably reached its lowest point. Estimates range between 375,000 and 500,000.

1901

President McKinley is assassinated by anarchist Leon Czolgosz. Theodore Roosevelt, age forty-two, becomes president.

> *"Now look! That damned cowboy is president of the United States!"*
>
> —Mark Hanna, adviser to President McKinley and senator from Ohio, speaking of Theodore Roosevelt

1902

President Roosevelt takes on the trusts, business combinations that restrain trade and competition.

The Sherman Antitrust Act, which Roosevelt invoked against trusts, had been passed in 1890 but had not been used with much success against business. Roosevelt argued, and the Supreme Court eventually agreed, that it wasn't the fact of corporate power that violated the Sherman Act, but the misuse of that power.

> *"We are not attacking the corporations, but endeavoring to do away with any evil in them."*
>
> —President Theodore Roosevelt

JOURNALISTS LIKE IDA TARBELL AND UPTON SINCLAIR, WHOM PRESIDENT ROOSEVELT LABELED MUCKRAKERS, POINTED OUT THE UNDERSIDE OF AMERICAN BUSINESS AND GAVE IMPETUS TO THE REFORMS HE SOUGHT.

"The men with the muck rakes are often indispensable to the well-being of society, but only if they know when to stop raking the muck."

—PRESIDENT THEODORE ROOSEVELT

1903

The Ford Motor Company is incorporated, with Henry Ford as vice president. The company sells its first car, the Model A.

1903

When the Colombian government blocks plans for a canal across the Colombian province of Panama, the United States supports a revolution that makes Panama an independent country. American steam shovels will be digging the canal the next year.

A FRENCH EFFORT TO BUILD A CANAL ACROSS THE ISTHMUS OF PANAMA FAILED BECAUSE THOUSANDS OF WORKMEN DIED OF YELLOW FEVER. THANKS TO THE KNOWLEDGE GAINED FROM MAJ. WALTER REED AND HIS VOLUNTEERS, THE UNITED STATES CARRIED OUT A PROGRAM OF MOSQUITO CONTROL AND KEPT THE AMERICAN PROJECT FROM SUFFERING THE FATE OF THE FRENCH.

1903

Wilbur and Orville Wright achieve the first sustained powered flight at Kitty Hawk, North Carolina.

THE WRIGHT BROTHERS AT KITTY HAWK, NORTH CAROLINA

1904

President Roosevelt, announcing a policy that will become known as the Roosevelt Corollary to the Monroe Doctrine, says that since the United States has forbidden European nations from intervening in Latin America, the U.S. must step in to keep order there when necessary.

1906

After more than fifty years of working for women's right to vote, Susan B. Anthony dies.

> "*Failure is impossible.*"
>
> —SUSAN B. ANTHONY, in her last public speech

ELIZABETH CADY STANTON, WHO, LIKE ANTHONY, WORKED TIRELESSLY FOR DECADES FOR A GOAL SHE DID NOT SEE REACHED, DIED BEFORE HER FRIEND SUSAN, IN 1902.

1906

President Roosevelt signs the American Antiquities Act. He will use the legislation to protect sites such as Devils Tower in Wyoming and the Grand Canyon in Arizona.

AN AVID HUNTER AND OUTDOORSMAN, ROOSEVELT WAS A DEDICATED CONSERVATIONIST. DURING HIS PRESIDENCY HE PLACED MORE THAN 225 MILLION ACRES OF LAND UNDER PUBLIC PROTECTION.

> *"There can be no greater issue than that of conservation in this country."*
>
> —PRESIDENT THEODORE ROOSEVELT in 1912

1907

Oklahoma joins the Union as the forty-sixth state.

1907

After mediating an end to a war between Russia and Japan, President Roosevelt decides to impress the Japanese (who have emerged as a power to be reckoned with), as well as the rest of the world, by sending the main part of the U.S. battle fleet around the globe.

> *"Speak softly and carry a big stick; you will go far."*
>
> —A West African proverb cited frequently by Theodore Roosevelt

PAINTED WHITE, THE SIXTEEN BATTLESHIPS OF THE U.S. FLEET WERE KNOWN AS THE GREAT WHITE FLEET. THEY RETURNED IN FEBRUARY 1909, JUST AS ROOSEVELT'S PRESIDENCY ENDED.

The Great White Fleet

"I *could not ask a finer concluding scene to my administrations.*"

—President Theodore Roosevelt

1908

During an era when the average number of immigrants entering the United States yearly is about one million, Israel Zangwill's play *The Melting Pot*, about the assimilation of new Americans, is a smash hit on Broadway.

"America is God's crucible, the great melting pot where all the races of Europe are melting and reforming!"

—Israel Zangwill

THE MELTING POT BECAME A CENTRAL METAPHOR FOR AMERICANIZATION PAGEANTS IN THE SECOND DECADE OF THE CENTURY. STUDENTS DRESSED IN NATIVE COSTUMES WOULD CLIMB INTO A "MELTING POT" AND EMERGE IN AMERICAN UNIFORMS—BOY SCOUT, RED CROSS NURSE, SOLDIER, SAILOR—THEN BE HANDED AN AMERICAN FLAG.

1908

William Howard Taft, Theodore Roosevelt's handpicked successor, is elected president.

1909

White and black leaders form the National Association for the Advancement of Colored People, an interracial organization dedicated to securing for African Americans the rights guaranteed by the Thirteenth, Fourteenth, and Fifteenth Amendments.

AMONG THOSE WHO HELPED FOUND THE NAACP WERE W. E. B. DU BOIS, WHO STARTED THE *CRISIS*, THE GROUP'S OFFICIAL PUBLICATION, AND IDA B. WELLS-BARNETT, WHO FOR NEARLY TWO DECADES HAD BEEN WORKING TO STOP THE LYNCHING OF AFRICAN-AMERICAN MEN.

1911

A fire breaks out at the Triangle Shirtwaist Company in lower Manhattan and kills 146 workers, most of them Jewish and Italian women. An investigating committee's recommendations will form the basis for better conditions for New York's factory workers.

Among those who witnessed desperate Triangle Shirtwaist workers jumping from the ninth and tenth floors of their building was twenty-eight-year-old Frances Perkins, who would one day become Franklin Delano Roosevelt's secretary of labor and the first woman cabinet member.

"[It was] *a never-to-be-forgotten reminder of why I had to spend my life fighting conditions that could permit such a tragedy.*"

—Frances Perkins, on the Triangle Shirtwaist fire

1911

The United States Supreme Court rules against the Standard Oil Trust and orders that it be dissolved.

The Taft administration supported the case against Standard Oil and initiated about twice as many antitrust actions as the Roosevelt administration had. But Taft did not like politics, lacked a gift for it, and managed to convey the impression that he was against progressive reforms, leading to a split in the Republican Party.

"Politics, when I am in it, makes me sick."

—William Howard Taft

1912

New Mexico joins the Union as the forty-seventh state.

1912

Arizona joins the Union as the forty-eighth state.

1912

The *Titanic*, thought by many to be unsinkable, hits an iceberg on her maiden voyage and sinks, killing more than fifteen hundred.

1912

Theodore Roosevelt, dissatisfied with Taft, runs against the president but loses the Republican nomination to him. Roosevelt bolts from the Republican Party and becomes the candidate of the Progressive, or Bull Moose Party.

A FANATIC APPROACHED ROOSEVELT AS HE WAS ON HIS WAY TO A CAMPAIGN EVENT AND SHOT HIM. THE BULLET WENT THROUGH HIS JACKET POCKET, SPECTACLES CASE, AND SPEECH BEFORE LODGING IN HIS CHEST. ROOSEVELT INSISTED ON PROCEEDING WITH HIS SPEECH, AND ONLY WHEN IT WAS OVER DID HE LET HIMSELF BE TAKEN TO THE HOSPITAL.

"It takes more than that to kill a Bull Moose."

—Theodore Roosevelt, showing his bloodstained shirt and holding up his bullet-torn speech

1912

Jim Thorpe, of Sauk and Fox heritage, wins both the decathlon and the pentathlon at the Olympics held in Stockholm, Sweden. In the same year he will lead the Carlisle Indian School football team to the national championship.

During years when Thorpe was playing Major League Baseball, he also led the Canton Bulldogs football team to three unofficial world championships.

"Sir, you are the greatest athlete in the world."

—King Gustav V of Sweden, to Jim Thorpe, who at the end of the century will be named athlete of the century

1912

With the Republican Party split, New Jersey governor Woodrow Wilson, a Democrat, is elected president of the United States.

Taft carried only two states in the 1912 election, Utah and Vermont. He would be appointed by President Warren G. Harding as chief justice of the Supreme Court and thus become the only man to reach the highest level of both the executive and the judicial branches.

THEODORE ROOSEVELT CONTINUED HIS EFFORTS TO PLAY A ROLE ON AMERICA'S GREAT STAGE, BUT NEVER AGAIN WOULD HE FIND A PART HE LOVED AS MUCH AS BEING PRESIDENT.

"It is not the critic who counts . . . [but] the man who is actually in the arena . . . ; who knows the great enthusiasms, the great devotions; who spends himself in a worthy cause; who at the best knows in the end the triumph of high achievement, and who at the worst, if he fails, at least fails while daring greatly, so that his place shall never be with those cold and timid souls who know neither victory nor defeat."

—PRESIDENT THEODORE ROOSEVELT

FIVE

FREEDOM FROM WANT, FREEDOM FROM FEAR

1913

The Sixteenth Amendment is ratified, giving Congress the power to establish a federal income tax.

1913

The Seventeenth Amendment is ratified, providing for the popular election of United States senators.

BEFORE THE RATIFICATION OF THE SEVENTEENTH AMENDMENT, STATE LEGISLATURES COULD SELECT A STATE'S SENATORS.

1913

President Woodrow Wilson, elected on a platform of "New Freedom," which promised economic reform, travels to Capitol Hill and urges Congress in his State of the Union address to pass antitrust legislation and to update the nation's archaic banking system.

PRESIDENTS HAD BECOME ACCUSTOMED TO SENDING WRITTEN STATE OF THE UNION MESSAGES, SO WHEN PRESIDENT WILSON WENT TO THE CAPITOL TO DELIVER HIS PERSONALLY, HE WAS THE FIRST CHIEF EXECUTIVE TO DO SO IN 113 YEARS. CONGRESS RESPONDED WITH A SPATE OF REFORM LEGISLATION: THE CLAYTON ANTITRUST ACT, THE FEDERAL TRADE COMMISSION ACT, THE FEDERAL RESERVE ACT, AND THE UNDERWOOD-SIMMONS TARIFF REDUCTION BILL.

1914

The assassination of Archduke Franz Ferdinand, heir to the Austro-Hungarian throne, leads to war in Europe, with Austria-Hungary, Germany, and the Ottoman Empire on one side, and the Allied powers, including Britain, France, and Russia, on the other. The United States adopts a position of neutrality.

> *"We must be impartial in thought, as well as action."*
> —PRESIDENT WOODROW WILSON

THE *LUSITANIA* DEPARTING NEW YORK ON HER LAST VOYAGE

1915

Germany, practicing a policy of unrestricted submarine warfare, sinks a British passenger liner, the *Lusitania*, killing 1,198, including 128 Americans. President Wilson responds angrily. Germany pledges publicly to stop attacking passenger ships without warning.

AFTER A SINGLE TORPEDO STRUCK THE *LUSITANIA*, A POWERFUL SECOND EXPLOSION HASTENED THE SHIP'S SINKING. MANY HAVE SPECULATED THAT CONTRABAND MUNITIONS IN THE SHIP'S MAGAZINE WERE RESPONSIBLE, BUT WHEN DR. ROBERT BALLARD (WHO FOUND THE *TITANIC*) EXAMINED THE WRECK OF THE *LUSITANIA*, HE DISCOVERED NO EVIDENCE OF AN EXPLOSION IN THE MAGAZINE. HE SPECULATED THAT COAL DUST CAUSED THE SECOND EXPLOSION.

1916

After the followers of Mexican revolutionary Pancho Villa kill dozens of Americans, President Wilson sends Gen. John J. Pershing and ten thousand troops to Mexico to capture him. American forces fail to find Villa and will return home the next year.

PRESIDENT WILSON HAD EARLIER INTERVENED IN MEXICAN AFFAIRS IN 1914 WHEN, IN AN EFFORT TO WEAKEN THE REGIME OF GEN. VICTORIANO HUERTA, HE SENT THE U.S. NAVY TO OCCUPY VERACRUZ. HE ALSO SENT MARINES INTO HAITI IN 1915 AND THE DOMINICAN REPUBLIC IN 1916 TO DEAL WITH DISTURBANCES IN THOSE COUNTRIES.

"*He kept us out of war.*"

—Democratic campaign slogan in 1916, emphasizing President Wilson's success in keeping the United States out of the war in Europe

1917

Recognizing their strategic importance, the U.S. purchases what will become the U.S. Virgin Islands from Denmark for $25 million.

1917

President Wilson signs the Jones-Shafroth Act. It establishes a locally elected senate and house of representatives in Puerto Rico (which was ceded to the United States after the Spanish-American War) and grants U.S. citizenship to Puerto Ricans.

1917

War sentiment grows after publication of the Zimmerman telegram, in which the German foreign minister proposes an alliance with Mexico. When Germany, having resumed unrestricted submarine warfare, torpedoes five American merchant ships, President Wilson delivers a war message and Congress declares war.

> *"We are glad, now that we see the facts . . . to fight thus for the ultimate peace of the world and for the liberation of its peoples, the German peoples included: for the rights of nations great and small and the privilege of men everywhere to choose their way of life. . . . The world must be made safe for democracy."*
>
> —President Woodrow Wilson

1917

The *Chicago Defender*, an influential black newspaper, declares May 15 the day of the Great Northern Drive as part of its effort to get African Americans in the South to move north. In the decades ahead millions of African Americans will move to urban centers in the North and West, in what will become known as the Great Migration.

1917

The Selective Service Act is passed, and the number of men in service begins to expand dramatically. Several hundred thousand strong at the beginning of the year, the armed forces will reach more than four million before war's end.

1917

Congress passes, and President Wilson signs, the Espionage Act, which will be followed by the Sedition Act of 1918, to impose fines and jail sentences on persons convicted of helping the country's enemies or interfering with the U.S. war effort.

> *"The question in every case is whether the words used are used in such circumstances and are of such a nature as to create a clear and present danger."*
>
> —Supreme Court justice OLIVER WENDELL HOLMES JR., writing for the Court in *Schenck v. United States*, a case brought under the Espionage Act

---

OF THE MORE THAN ONE THOUSAND PEOPLE CONVICTED UNDER THE ESPIONAGE AND SEDITION ACTS, MORE THAN ONE HUNDRED WERE LATER GRANTED CLEMENCY, INCLUDING SOCIALIST LEADER EUGENE DEBS. ONE WHO WAS NOT PARDONED WAS BILL HAYWOOD, A LEADER OF THE INDUSTRIAL WORKERS OF THE WORLD, WHO JUMPED BAIL AND FLED TO MOSCOW, WHERE HE DIED IN 1928. HALF HIS ASHES WERE BURIED IN THE KREMLIN, THE OTHER HALF IN CHICAGO NEAR A MONUMENT TO THE HAYMARKET ANARCHISTS.

1917

The first American troops arrive in France.

> *"Lafayette, we are here."*
>
> —LT. COL. CHARLES STANTON

SUFFRAGISTS MARCHING FOR THE VOTE

1917

Alice Paul and other advocates of a constitutional amendment that will recognize women's right to vote demonstrate outside the White House and are arrested. They will later be released and their convictions overturned, but not before Paul spends time in solitary confinement, goes on a hunger strike, and is force-fed.

> *"Democracy should begin at home."*
>
> —Message on a banner carried outside the White House by one of the suffragists

1918

In an address to Congress, President Woodrow Wilson sets forth the war aims of the United States. Among the fourteen points he makes: the necessity for freedom of the seas, for reduction in armaments, and for an association of nations.

> "*A general association of nations must be formed under specific covenants for the purpose of affording mutual guarantees of political independence and territorial integrity to great and small states alike.*"
>
> —President Woodrow Wilson

1918

At Belleau Wood, in France, American forces stop the German advance toward Paris.

A poster urging Americans to support the war

"Retreat? Hell, we just got here."

—An American marine, replying to a suggestion at Belleau Wood that he and his men fall back

1918

President Wilson sends troops to Russia, where the Bolsheviks have seized power and murdered Czar Nicholas II and his family. The Americans support the anti-Bolshevik forces, but their intervention will fail.

1918

More than a million American fighting men push through the Argonne Forest. Ultimately the Allies break through the German line.

As the Allies were launching their final offensive, a new enemy emerged: a deadly flu virus. It killed upward of 50 million, including approximately 675,000 Americans. Roughly 50,000 Americans were killed in combat in World War I.

1918

The Germans seek an end to fighting, Germany's Kaiser Wilhelm abdicates, and an armistice is declared.

The war ended at 11:00 a.m. on the eleventh day of the eleventh month. For many years November 11 was celebrated as Armistice Day, but in 1954 the day became known as Veterans Day. It honors all who have served in the United States armed forces.

1919

The Eighteenth Amendment, prohibiting the making, selling, or transport of alcoholic beverages, is ratified. It will prove hard to enforce, bootleg liquor will become a source of revenue for organized crime, and fourteen years later the amendment will be repealed.

1919

In the midst of labor turmoil, some thirty bombs are mailed to public figures across the country, including Seattle mayor Ole Hanson, who has fiercely opposed a general strike in that city and been an outspoken opponent of communism and anarchism.

NO ONE WAS KILLED BY THE BOMBS, THOUGH ONE WOMAN LOST HER HANDS. MORE THAN A DOZEN BOMBS NEVER REACHED THEIR INTENDED TARGETS BECAUSE THE SENDERS DID NOT PUT SUFFICIENT POSTAGE ON THEM.

1919

Bombs go off in eight cities, including Washington, D.C., where an explosion destroys the front of Attorney General A. Mitchell Palmer's house. Palmer will lead an effort to round up and deport thousands of suspected Bolsheviks and anarchists.

AMID RISING PROTEST THAT HE WAS VIOLATING CIVIL LIBERTIES, ATTORNEY GENERAL PALMER PREDICTED AN UPRISING OF RADICALS ON MAY DAY 1920. WHEN IT DID NOT MATERIALIZE, HIS CREDIBILITY SUFFERED. THE RED SCARE SUBSIDED, BUT IT DID NOT GO AWAY.

THE FOLLOWING SEPTEMBER THERE WAS ANOTHER BOMBING, THIS ONE ON WALL STREET. AT LEAST THIRTY PEOPLE WERE KILLED, AND MANY MORE WERE INJURED. IN DECEMBER 249 RADICALS—ANARCHIST EMMA GOLDMAN AMONG THEM—WERE DEPORTED TO THE SOVIET UNION ABOARD THE SS *BUFORD*, WHICH BECAME WIDELY KNOWN AS THE RED ARK.

1919

The Treaty of Versailles is signed, formally ending the war. At European insistence the treaty provides that Germany make large reparations for losses inflicted by war. At President Woodrow Wilson's insistence provisions are included for the League of Nations.

WHEN PRESIDENT WILSON WENT TO FRANCE TO NEGOTIATE THE TREATY OF VERSAILLES, HE BECAME THE FIRST PRESIDENT TO TRAVEL TO EUROPE WHILE IN OFFICE. THE SHIP ON WHICH HE SAILED, THE *GEORGE WASHINGTON*, HAD FORMERLY BEEN A GERMAN PASSENGER LINER.

"Dare we reject it and break the heart of the world?"

—PRESIDENT WOODROW WILSON, presenting the Treaty of Versailles to the United States Senate

"The United States is the world's best hope, but if you fetter her in the interests and quarrels of other nations, if you tangle her in the intrigues of Europe, you will destroy her power for good, and endanger

her very existence. Leave her to march freely through the centuries to come, as in the years that have gone."

—Senator Henry Cabot Lodge, opposing the provision for the League of Nations in the Treaty of Versailles

1919

In the wake of the Bolshevik Revolution, the Communist Party of the United States of America is founded as part of the Communist International. Its purpose is to bring about the downfall of capitalism and to establish the dictatorship of the proletariat.

"*A new era in world history has begun. Mankind is throwing off the last form of slavery: capitalist, or wage, slavery.*"

—Vladimir Ilyich Lenin

1919

After Congress balks at the Treaty of Versailles, particularly at provisions for the League of Nations, President Woodrow Wilson, refusing to compromise, launches a cross-country tour to present his case to the people. He will become ill on the trip, return to the White House, and suffer a massive stroke.

After President Wilson's stroke his second wife, Edith Bolling Wilson, controlled access to him, decided with his secretary, Joseph Tumulty, what documents he should see, and conveyed his orders to the outside world. But there is no evidence that she made

HIS DECISIONS. INDEED, WHEN SHE SUGGESTED HE COMPROMISE ON THE TREATY OF VERSAILLES, HE IGNORED HER ADVICE.

PRESIDENT WILSON PROMOTING THE LEAGUE OF NATIONS

1919

The Senate fails to approve the Treaty of Versailles. In another vote the next year, the Senate will again fail to approve the treaty.

1920

The Nineteenth Amendment, recognizing women's right to vote, is ratified.

> *"The right of citizens of the United States to vote shall not be denied or abridged by the United States or by any state on account of sex."*
>
> –The Nineteenth Amendment

"We are no longer petitioners. We are not wards of the nation, but free and equal citizens."

—Carrie Chapman Catt, president of the National American Woman Suffrage Association

Lining up to vote in 1920

1920

Warren G. Harding, a Republican, promising an era of peace and stability, is elected president of the United States.

"America's present need is not heroics, but healing; not nostrums, but normalcy; not revolution, but restoration."

—Warren G. Harding, campaigning for president

1921

Nicola Sacco and Bartolomeo Vanzetti, arrested for killing two in a robbery attempt, are put on trial and sentenced to death. Their conviction and execution bring a passionate outcry from those who believe they are being punished because they are militant anarchists rather than because they are guilty of the crimes for which they were charged.

> *"all right we are two nations."*
>
> —John Dos Passos, U.S.A., expressing the anger of those who believe Sacco and Vanzetti were wrongly convicted

---

In 1983 forensics experts reevaluated firearms evidence from the Sacco and Vanzetti trial and concluded that one of the fatal bullets was fired from a Colt .32 automatic taken from Sacco.

Historian Paul Avrich, who has written extensively about anarchism, concludes it is a "virtual certainty" that Sacco and Vanzetti were involved in the 1919 bombings.

1923

President Warren G. Harding, plagued by rumors of scandals in his administration, dies in California while on his way back from Alaska. He is succeeded by Vice President Calvin Coolidge.

The Teapot Dome scandal was the biggest of the Harding years. It involved Secretary of the Interior Albert Fall, who leased federal oil lands to friends in exchange for cash and gifts. Fall was fined and imprisoned.

1924

The National Origins Act establishes fixed quotas for immigration based on national origin. It becomes particularly difficult for eastern and southern Europeans to immigrate, and impossible for those from Asia.

1924

The Indian Citizenship Act makes all Indians born in the United States citizens.

Even after the Indian Citizenship Act, some states withheld the right to vote. It was nearly forty years before Indian voting rights were recognized across the nation.

1924

Calvin Coolidge, who became president upon Warren G. Harding's death, is elected in his own right. Times are generally prosperous, and his vote total is greater than that of both his opponents: Senator Robert La Follette of Wisconsin, who broke from the Republican party to run as the Progressive candidate, and John Davis, the Democratic nominee.

> *"You lose."*
>
> —President Calvin Coolidge, according to legend, responding to a woman who said, "Mr. President, I made a bet I could get more than two words out of you."

The size of the federal government over which President Coolidge presided was small, about 3 percent of the gross domestic

PRODUCT, AS COMPARED WITH 20 PERCENT IN 2004. AS FRUGAL WITH THE TAXPAYERS' MONEY AS HE WAS WITH WORDS, PRESIDENT COOLIDGE HAD NO INTEREST IN SEEING THE FEDERAL GOVERNMENT GROW LARGER.

1925

In Tennessee, where the teaching of evolution in public schools has been outlawed, the American Civil Liberties Union sponsors a test case that puts science teacher John Scopes on trial. Famed Chicago lawyer and agnostic Clarence Darrow defends him; former secretary of state and three-time presidential candidate William Jennings Bryan, a devout Christian, is part of the team that prosecutes the case.

AFTER THE JUDGE INSTRUCTED THE JURY THAT THE ONLY QUESTION FOR THEM TO DECIDE WAS WHETHER SCOPES HAD BROKEN THE STATE LAW PROHIBITING THE TEACHING OF EVOLUTION, A VERDICT OF GUILTY WAS ASSURED. THUS, *TENNESSEE V. SCOPES*, THOUGH OFTEN CALLED THE TRIAL OF THE CENTURY, DID NOT SETTLE MUCH. IT DID, HOWEVER, PROVIDE OCCASION FOR DARROW AND BRYAN TO MAKE POWERFUL STATEMENTS OF THEIR CASES.

> *"Here, we find today as brazen and as bold an attempt to destroy learning as was ever made in the Middle Ages, and the only difference is we have not provided that they shall be burned at the stake."*
>
> —Clarence Darrow

> *"Religion is not hostile to learning. . . . Christianity welcomes truth from whatever source it comes. . . . Evolution is not truth; it is merely an hypothesis—it is millions of guesses strung together."*
>
> —WILLIAM JENNINGS BRYAN

CHARLES LINDBERGH

1927

Charles Lindbergh flies a single-engine plane, the *Spirit of St. Louis,* from Roosevelt Field on Long Island to Le Bourget Airport near Paris, becoming the first person to fly solo nonstop across the Atlantic.

> *"I flew low over the field once, then circled around into the wind and landed."*
>
> —CHARLES LINDBERGH

LINDBERGH FLEW WITHOUT A PARACHUTE OR A RADIO SO THAT HE COULD CARRY MORE GASOLINE.

1928

After Calvin Coolidge unexpectedly decides not to run for president again, Herbert Hoover, a Republican, is elected.

An engineer and humanitarian, Hoover came into office with a reputation for being a man of good character, great intelligence, and formidable organizational skills. In 1919, Assistant Secretary of the Navy Franklin D. Roosevelt offered him high praise.

> *"He is certainly a wonder and I wish we could make him president of the United States. There could not be a better one."*
>
> —Franklin D. Roosevelt

1928

Shortly after his election Hoover takes a weeks-long tour of Latin America, during which he makes clear that he will work to improve relations between the United States and countries to its south.

> *"We have a desire to maintain not only the cordial relations of governments with each other but the relations of good neighbors."*
>
> —President-elect Herbert Hoover

1929

After a spectacular climb the stock market crashes. The plunge begins on Black Thursday, October 24, and accelerates as people who have purchased stock with borrowed money are forced to sell. By the end of trading on Black Tuesday, October 29, some $32 billion has been lost, an amount greater than the U.S. spent on World War I.

> *"Life would no longer be, ever again, all fun and games. The bam-bang-sock-and-pow part was over, and so was the permanent, floating New Year's Eve party."*
>
> —HARPO MARX, comedian and stock market investor

WALL STREET ON BLACK THURSDAY

BY CLOSE OF MARKET ON OCTOBER 29, THE DOW JONES AVERAGE WAS AT 230.07, DOWN 40 PERCENT FROM ITS SEPTEMBER HIGH OF 381.17. THE MARKET RALLIED IN THE SPRING, BUT THEN THINGS GOT WORSE—MUCH WORSE. IN 1932 THE DOW JONES AVERAGE HIT A LOW OF 41.22, DOWN 90 PERCENT FROM ITS 1929 PEAK.

1930

President Hoover, fulfilling a campaign pledge to help farmers, signs the Hawley-Smoot Tariff Act, a measure that raises duties on imports to historic levels.

CONCERNED THAT THE HAWLEY-SMOOT TARIFF WOULD LEAD TO A DRASTIC SLOWDOWN IN INTERNATIONAL TRADE AND FURTHER WEAKEN THE U.S. ECONOMY, ONE THOUSAND ECONOMISTS SIGNED A PETITION URGING PRESIDENT HOOVER TO VETO THE BILL. HE ARGUED THAT PROVISIONS IN THE LAW COULD OVERCOME ITS WEAKNESSES AND NOTED AS WELL THAT HE HAD PROMISED SUCH A MEASURE IN THE 1928 CAMPAIGN.

"Platform promises must not be empty gestures."
—PRESIDENT HERBERT HOOVER

1930

As depression begins to set in on the American economy, banks start to fail in record numbers. As depositors demand their money, banks call in loans. Farm foreclosures follow.

1931

Japan invades Manchuria, violating agreements to which the United States is party, but the U.S. does not respond forcefully, nor does the League of Nations.

1932

In an effort to shore up the financial system, including farm mortgage associations and agricultural credit bureaus as well as railroads and banks, President Hoover creates the Reconstruction Finance Corporation.

AS THE NUMBER OF UNEMPLOYED TOPPED TEN MILLION, PRESIDENT HOOVER PROVIDED FUNDS FOR PUBLIC WORKS PROJECTS AND A SMALL AMOUNT FOR RELIEF PROGRAMS TO BE RUN BY STATES, BUT HE WAS CONCERNED THAT SUCH PROGRAMS, IF THEY BECAME PERMANENT, COULD MAKE INDIVIDUALS TOO DEPENDENT ON GOVERNMENT. THE DEMOCRATIC GOVERNOR OF NEW YORK LOOKED AT IT DIFFERENTLY.

"[Help to jobless citizens] must be extended by government, not as a matter of charity, but as a matter of social duty."

—FRANKLIN DELANO ROOSEVELT, governor of New York

GOVERNOR FRANKLIN DELANO ROOSEVELT CAMPAIGNING

1932

Roosevelt becomes the Democratic nominee for president.

"I pledge you, I pledge myself, to a new deal for the American people."

—Franklin D. Roosevelt

Depression-era unemployed

1932

Unemployed veterans march on Washington to lobby for early payment of a bonus due them; riots ensue, and President Hoover calls in troops. Gen. Douglas MacArthur, exceeding his orders, uses cavalry to charge the marchers, drives them from their tent city, and burns it.

1933

After defeating Hoover, Roosevelt takes the oath of office as president of the United States.

"The only thing we have to fear is fear itself."

—President Franklin D. Roosevelt, in his inaugural address

Just a little more than a month before FDR took the inaugural oath, Adolf Hitler became chancellor of the German Reich.

1933

The day after his inauguration, President Roosevelt, faced with banking panics across the country, declares a bank holiday. While the banks are closed, he delivers his first radio "fireside chat," reassuring Americans that their banks are safe. When the banks reopen, deposits begin to flow back into them.

"There is an element in the readjustment of our financial system more important than currency, more important than gold, and that is the confidence of the people."

—President Franklin D. Roosevelt

1933

President Roosevelt sends fifteen messages to Congress and signs fifteen bills in what becomes known as the first Hundred Days. Measures become law that deal with farm problems; put men to work in flood control, forestry, and irrigation; and create the Tennessee Valley Authority to electrify and improve the Tennessee River watershed. The National Industrial Recovery Act creates a public works program, establishes a system for controlling prices and production, and gives an important boost to the union movement.

1934

Socialist- and Communist-led strikes lead to violence in Toledo, Ohio; San Francisco, California; and Minneapolis, Minnesota. Labor succeeds in getting key demands met.

1934

The Indian Reorganization Act, sometimes called the Indian New Deal, becomes law. It tries to protect the holdings of Native-American reservations by encouraging tribal ownership. Many tribes vote not to participate.

1934

Triggered by drought, dust storms sweep across wide portions of the country. Hard-hit tenant farmers from Arkansas, Oklahoma, and other states begin to head west, looking for a way to make a living.

A farm in the dust bowl

> *"In the souls of the people, the grapes of wrath are filling and growing heavy, growing heavy for the vintage."*
>
> —John Steinbeck, *The Grapes of Wrath*, a novel about men and women leaving the dust bowl during the Great Depression

1935

President Franklin D. Roosevelt creates the Works Progress Administration, which pays people to undertake many activities, from building roads to writing guidebooks.

1935

In *Schechter Poultry Corporation v. United States*, the Supreme Court declares the National Industrial Recovery Act, a centerpiece of the New Deal, unconstitutional. The Court will also strike down the Agricultural Adjustment Act.

1935

President Roosevelt signs the Wagner Act, which makes it easier to organize unions, and the Social Security Act, which provides benefits for old age, financed by taxes on workers and employers.

For the most part the legislative phase of the New Deal was over. President Roosevelt had redefined the role of government in American life, but millions remained unemployed. For the rest of the decade, yearly unemployment rates remained above 14 percent.

1936

The Democrats nominate President Roosevelt for a second term.

> *"There is a mysterious cycle in human events. To some generations much is given. Of other generations much is expected. This generation of Americans has a rendezvous with destiny."*
>
> —President Franklin D. Roosevelt, accepting the Democratic nomination

1937

After a resounding reelection victory President Roosevelt is sworn in for a second time.

> *"I see one third of a nation ill-housed, ill-clad, ill-nourished. It is not in despair that I paint you that picture. I paint it for you in hope—because the nation, seeing and understanding the injustice in it, proposes to paint it out."*
>
> —President Franklin D. Roosevelt

1937

President Roosevelt attempts to gain control over the Supreme Court, which he sees as a threat to New Deal legislation. He puts forward a plan to increase the number of justices, but his attempt at "Court packing" draws widespread opposition.

Although President Roosevelt did not change the number of justices in the Court, some have suggested that he may have changed their opinions. In 1937 the Court

ISSUED A NUMBER OF DECISIONS FAVORABLE TO THE NEW DEAL, INCLUDING RULINGS THAT UPHELD BOTH THE WAGNER ACT AND THE LEGISLATION CREATING SOCIAL SECURITY.

1937

The Japanese launch an all-out war on China, causing President Roosevelt to speak out against "the epidemic of world lawlessness."

THE PRESIDENT'S SPEECH DREW HARSH REVIEWS FROM ISOLATIONISTS, WHOSE VIEWS REPRESENTED THE BELIEFS OF MANY AMERICANS. A PUBLIC-OPINION POLL CONDUCTED IN 1938 ASKED, "IF ENGLAND AND FRANCE GO TO WAR AGAINST GERMANY, DO YOU THINK THIS COUNTRY SHOULD DECLARE WAR ON GERMANY?" NINETY PERCENT ANSWERED NO.

ADOLF HITLER IN VIENNA, AUSTRIA

1938

Adolf Hitler annexes Austria and begins to persecute that country's Jewish population in the same ways he has persecuted Jews in Germany. Quota restrictions in U.S. immigration law make it difficult for Jews to escape Nazi oppression by coming to America.

THE SS *ST. LOUIS*, A SHIP WITH NEARLY A THOUSAND JEWISH REFUGEES ABOARD, SAILED TO WITHIN SIGHT OF THE UNITED STATES. WHEN PASSENGERS WERE NOT ALLOWED TO DISEMBARK AT ANY PORT, THE SHIP RETURNED TO EUROPE.

1938

As America watches, representatives of Britain and France meet with Hitler in Munich and sign an agreement ceding the Sudetenland, part of Czechoslovakia, to Germany.

> "*I believe it is peace in our time.*"
>
> —British prime minister NEVILLE CHAMBERLAIN

IN LESS THAN SIX MONTHS HITLER CONTROLLED MOST OF CZECHOSLOVAKIA.

1939

When the Daughters of the American Revolution refuse to let renowned contralto Marian Anderson appear in Constitution Hall because she is black, Eleanor Roosevelt resigns from the organization, and Anderson sings from the steps of the Lincoln Memorial before 75,000 people gathered on the mall.

MARIAN ANDERSON PERFORMING AT THE LINCOLN MEMORIAL

1939

Hitler, having concluded a nonaggression pact with the Soviet Union, invades Poland, causing Britain and France to declare war on Germany. A few weeks later the Red Army moves into the eastern part of Poland, leaving that country divided between Nazi and Communist forces.

> *"This nation will remain a neutral nation, but I cannot ask that every American remain neutral in thought as well."*
>
> —PRESIDENT FRANKLIN D. ROOSEVELT, in a fireside chat

1940

Overcoming determined Finnish resistance, the Soviets take substantial portions of Finland, and they occupy the Baltic states. In a blitzkrieg, or "lightning war," Hitler's army overruns Denmark, Norway, the Netherlands,

Belgium, and Luxembourg. Soon France, too, falls. Germany begins to bomb England.

1940

President Roosevelt arranges to provide destroyers to Britain, and Congress passes the country's first peacetime draft.

> *"We must be the great arsenal of democracy."*
>
> —President Franklin D. Roosevelt, in a fireside chat

1940

Breaking all precedent, Roosevelt runs for and wins a third term as president.

1941

In his State of the Union message, President Roosevelt asks Congress to pass the Lend-Lease Act, a program allowing the United States to lend or lease war materials to other countries, and he sets forth his goals for America and the world.

> *"In the future days, which we seek to make secure, we look forward to a world founded upon four essential human freedoms. The first is freedom of speech and expression. . . . The second is freedom of every person to worship God in his own way. . . . The third is freedom from want. . . . The fourth is freedom from fear."*
>
> —President Franklin D. Roosevelt

1941

In a move that will have enormous consequences, Hitler breaks the nonaggression pact with the Soviet Union and invades the USSR. The Soviet Union will become an ally of the United States and Britain.

THE ATTACK ON PEARL HARBOR

1941

The Japanese attack Pearl Harbor, destroying U.S. battleships and killing some 2,400 Americans.

> *"Yesterday, December 7, 1941—a date which will live in infamy—the United States of America was suddenly and deliberately attacked by naval and air forces of the empire of Japan."*
>
> —PRESIDENT FRANKLIN D. ROOSEVELT, war message to Congress

1941

On December 8 the United States declares war on Japan. Within a few days the U.S. will be at war with Germany and Italy as well.

1942

President Roosevelt creates the War Production Board to focus the nation's economy on wartime production. By the time the war ends, America's factories will have produced nearly 300,000 aircraft, more than 70,000 ships, and 85,000 tanks.

Millions of women went to work in offices and factories as men left their jobs to fight in the war. Women also joined the army, navy, Marine Corps, coast guard, and army air forces.

Women factory workers

1942

American submarines begin to operate against Japanese warships and merchant ships, and will take a heavy toll. The Silent Service, as it is called, is also a dangerous service: About one submarine out of four does not return.

1942

President Roosevelt signs Executive Order 9066, allowing Americans of Japanese descent to be interned in areas away from the West Coast.

Thousands of Japanese Americans served in the United States armed forces. The 442nd Regimental Combat Team, a Japanese-American unit, became one of the most decorated in military history.

1942

President Roosevelt orders Gen. Douglas MacArthur to leave the Philippines, which are under Japanese onslaught.

> "I *shall return*."
>
> —Gen. Douglas MacArthur

As the Japanese marched toward Manila, American and Filipino soldiers withdrew to the Bataan Peninsula. When the Japanese captured it, they forced American and Filipino soldiers on a sixty-five-mile march—long known as the Bataan Death March—that killed as many as ten thousand.

1942

After capturing a vast empire in the Pacific, the Japanese move toward Australia; a U.S. carrier fleet blocks their way in the Battle of the Coral Sea. A month later the Japanese attack Midway Island, where they find the Americans waiting for them. U.S. bombers sink four of the six Japanese carriers that attacked Pearl Harbor and turn the tide of war in the Pacific theater.

Having partially broken a code that the Japanese were using, American forces were aware that an attack was planned on "AF." Suspecting that might refer to Midway, intelligence officers had the American garrison there transmit a message about being low on water. When Japanese transmissions began to refer to AF as low on water, the Americans knew the Japanese target.

The U.S. had a code that the Japanese never deciphered. It was created by Navajo "code-talkers" who served as Marine communicators in the Pacific and transmitted messages using their native language.

1942

U.S. Marines invade Guadalcanal, beginning a long march across the Pacific to take back lands conquered by the Japanese.

"What I'd give for a piece of blueberry pie."

—A marine on Guadalcanal, when asked by journalist John Hersey, "What are you fighting for?"

"In other places there are other symbols. . . . A good bottle of scotch . . . a blonde . . . books . . . movies. . . . When they say they are fighting for these things, they mean that they are fighting for home."

—JOHN HERSEY, journalist

1942

U.S. forces land in North Africa, beginning a campaign with the British that will drive the Germans and Italians out of North Africa the following year.

1943

After a year of hitting targets in France and the Low Countries, B-17s flying out of England bomb targets in Germany.

THE EARLY FORAYS INTO GERMANY EXACTED A FEARFUL COST: IN A SINGLE RAID SIXTY BOMBERS WERE LOST. THEN P-51 MUSTANGS—LONG-RANGE FIGHTER PLANES—BEGAN ACCOMPANYING B-17 AND B-24 BOMBERS AND PROVIDING PROTECTION. BOMBER CREWS CALLED THE MUSTANG "LITTLE FRIEND."

1943

After capturing Sicily, American forces invade Italy and start a campaign up the peninsula that will last until the spring of 1945.

"I dove in behind one plane as he flew level. He started maneuvering a little bit, I started shooting, and the airplane started coming apart . . . and exploded."

—Lt. Clarence Lester, 332nd Fighter Group, which escorted bombers based in Italy

The men of the 332nd, all African American, had trained at Tuskegee Institute in Alabama. They compiled an admirable record, not losing a single bomber that they escorted and winning 150 Distinguished Flying Crosses.

Cadets at Tuskegee Institute

Benito Mussolini, the Fascist dictator of Italy, was deposed as American troops made their way across Sicily. Italy then entered the war on the side of the Allies, but the Germans

WERE FIRMLY ENTRENCHED. ON JUNE 4, 1944, NEARLY A YEAR AFTER THE INVASION OF SICILY, THE FIFTH ARMY ENTERED ROME.

1944

After a major buildup of forces in England, Allied forces invade the continent of Europe on June 6, D-Day. More than 175,000 men launch the assault. Four thousand ships and more than eleven thousand planes are involved.

GEN. DWIGHT D. EISENHOWER WAS IN COMMAND OF THE INVASION. IN HIS POCKET HE CARRIED A MESSAGE ACCEPTING BLAME, WHICH HE INTENDED TO RELEASE SHOULD THE INVASION FAIL, BUT IT SUCCEEDED AND MADE HIM A HERO.

1944

Paris is liberated.

ADOLF HITLER GAVE ORDERS TO DESTROY MAJOR BUILDINGS AND BRIDGES IN PARIS, BUT GEN. DIETRICH VON CHOLTITZ REFUSED TO FOLLOW THOSE INSTRUCTIONS AND INSTEAD ARRANGED A SURRENDER THAT PROVIDED FOR WITHDRAWING THE OCCUPYING FORCES AND LEAVING THE CITY UNHARMED.

1944

After the Majdanek concentration camp is captured by the Red Army, reporters begin to bring the story of the Holocaust to the world. More than eight hundred thousand pairs of shoes are found at the camp.

AFTER THE WAR AN INTERNATIONAL WAR CRIMES TRIBUNAL CHARGED NAZI LEADERS WITH CRIMES AGAINST HUMANITY. TWELVE WERE SENTENCED TO DEATH, AND ELEVEN WERE HANGED. ONE, HERMANN GÖRING, COMMITTED SUICIDE BEFORE HE WAS TO BE EXECUTED.

"If, after all this suffering, there are still Jews left, the Jewish people will be held up as an example. Who knows, maybe our religion will teach the world and all the people in it about goodness, and that's the reason, the only reason, we have to suffer."

—ANNE FRANK, who died in the Bergen-Belsen concentration camp

CONCENTRATION CAMP AT DACHAU AFTER LIBERATION BY AMERICAN SOLDIERS

1944

After several successful island campaigns in the Pacific, U.S. Army and Navy forces invade the Philippines. In the Battle of

Leyte Gulf, the Japanese use kamikazes, or suicide bombers, for the first time, but they do not turn the tide of battle.

> *"People of the Philippines: I have returned."*
>
> —GEN. DOUGLAS MACARTHUR, after wading ashore

1944–45

As Allied forces approach, Germany launches a major effort to halt their advance. German troops push a part of the Allied line back, creating a "bulge" that gives the Battle of the Bulge its name. Ultimately the Allies restore the line, overcoming the last major German offensive action in the west.

1945

President Franklin D. Roosevelt, British prime minister Winston Churchill, and Soviet premier Joseph Stalin meet at Yalta in the Crimea. The agreements they reach about postwar Europe will have a profound effect on the years ahead.

PRIME MINISTER WINSTON CHURCHILL, PRESIDENT FRANKLIN ROOSEVELT, AND PREMIER JOSEPH STALIN AT YALTA

THE GERMAN INVASION OF POLAND HAD STARTED WORLD WAR II. NOW THE SOVIETS OCCUPIED THAT COUNTRY. STALIN PLEDGED TO HOLD "FREE AND UNFETTERED" ELECTIONS IN POLAND AS SOON AS POSSIBLE AND SIGNED A DECLARATION COMMITTING TO FREE ELECTIONS FOR ALL LIBERATED PEOPLES, BUT NONE OF THESE PROMISES WERE KEPT.

> *"There is a good deal of uneasiness in both parties that we are letting the Poles down."*
>
> —PRIME MINISTER WINSTON CHURCHILL, to President Franklin D. Roosevelt

1945

U.S. Marines take Iwo Jima, where Japanese airfields and radar stations have been a hindrance to the American bombing campaign being conducted by B-29 Superfortresses against Japanese cities.

> *"We stuck together. You never let a buddy down. You did your job. You did it well. You were proud of your outfit, proud of the Corps, proud of your country. We knew that we could take Iwo Jima and we did. We paid for it with our blood."*
>
> —GEORGE ELDER, U.S. Marines

1945

Undertaking what will be one of the bloodiest battles of the war in the Pacific, U.S. forces invade Okinawa, an island less than four hundred miles from the home islands of Japan.

By the time the battle was over and the Americans had won, seventy thousand Japanese and one hundred thousand Okinawans were dead. Thirty-nine thousand Americans who had fought on the island were killed, wounded, or missing in action, as were another ten thousand at sea, where the Japanese had launched fierce kamikaze attacks on U.S. ships.

1945

President Roosevelt dies in Warm Springs, Georgia. Harry S. Truman becomes president of the United States.

1945

Delegates from fifty nations meet in San Francisco and draw up the charter for the United Nations. The organization will hold its first meeting the next year.

1945

On May 7, Germany surrenders unconditionally. Across all the Allied countries there is joy.

1945

President Harry S. Truman—in Potsdam, Germany, to meet with Allied leaders—learns that a powerful new weapon has been successfully tested. Believing that an invasion of Japan will cost hundreds of thousands of American lives, the president decides to use the new weapon, and on August 6 an American bomber, the *Enola Gay*, drops an atomic bomb on Hiroshima. On August 9 another atomic weapon is dropped on Nagasaki. In these two cities more than a hundred thousand are killed immediately.

"We turned back to look at Hiroshima. The city was hidden by that awful cloud . . . , boiling up, mushrooming, terrible and incredibly tall."

—COL. PAUL W. TIBBETS JR., pilot of the *Enola Gay*

1945

On August 14, America learns that the Japanese will surrender. Church bells ring across the country.

"I feel like I've played my part in turning this from a century of darkness into a century of light."

—An American GI, upon being asked by author Stephen Ambrose, "Was it worth it?"

NEW YORK, AFTER THE JAPANESE SURRENDER IS ANNOUNCED

SIX

FIGHTING FOR FREEDOM AT HOME AND ABROAD

1946

GIs returning home find jobs in an expanding economy. Using the GI Bill, millions will go back to school and buy homes.

THE GI BILL, WHICH PRESIDENT FRANKLIN D. ROOSEVELT SIGNED SHORTLY AFTER D-DAY IN 1944, PROVIDED TUITION AND LIVING EXPENSES FOR VETERANS GOING TO SCHOOL OR SEEKING TRAINING. BY THE TIME THE DECADE WAS OVER, NEARLY NINE MILLION GIS HAD TAKEN ADVANTAGE OF IT.

1946

Introduced by President Harry S. Truman, former British prime minister Winston Churchill delivers a speech at Westminster College in Fulton, Missouri, in which he warns about the ambitions of Soviet Russia and urges Western democracies to stand strong.

> *"From Stettin in the Baltic to Trieste in the Adriatic, an iron curtain has descended across the Continent. . . . From what I have seen of our Russian friends and Allies during the war, I am convinced that there is nothing they admire so much as strength, and there is nothing for which they have less respect than for weakness, especially military weakness."*
>
> —WINSTON CHURCHILL

1946

Republicans sweep the off-year elections, coming into control of both the House and the Senate for the first time since the Great Depression.

Among the new members of the House of Representatives were Richard Nixon of California and John Kennedy of Massachusetts. Joseph McCarthy of Wisconsin was a freshman member of the Senate.

1947

When Great Britain announces that it can no longer afford to provide military and economic aid to Greece and Turkey, President Harry S. Truman appears before Congress to request funds for both countries so that they do not fall into Communist hands.

> "*I believe that it must be the policy of the* United States *to support free peoples who are resisting attempted subjugation by armed minorities or by outside pressures.*"
>
> —President Harry S. Truman, announcing what will become known as the Truman Doctrine

---

The president's speech was part of a developing bipartisan response to the Soviet Union that would be called "containment." The point of the strategy was to block further expansion of Soviet power and influence.

1947

The House Un-American Activities Committee (HUAC) begins investigating Communist influence in the motion picture industry. Among those who will testify is Screen Actors Guild president Ronald Reagan, who has resigned from two groups influenced by the Communist Party.

> "*I detest, I abhor their philosophy, but I detest more than that their tactics, which are those of a fifth column, and are dishonest, but at the same time I never as a citizen want to see our country . . . , by either fear or resentment of this group, . . . ever compromise with any of our democratic principles.*"
>
> —RONALD REAGAN

AS SCREEN ACTORS GUILD PRESIDENT, REAGAN URGED OTHER ACTORS TO VOLUNTEER TO APPEAR BEFORE HUAC, BUT HE ALSO NOTED THAT SOME COMMITTEE MEMBERS, "IGNORING STANDARDS OF TRUTH AND FAIR PLAY, GANGED UP ON INNOCENT PEOPLE AND TRIED TO BLACKLIST THEM."

1947

President Harry S. Truman signs an executive order making all federal employees subject to loyalty investigations.

> "*I am not worried about the Communist Party taking over the government of the United States, but I am against a person, whose loyalty is not to the government of the United States, holding a government job.*"
>
> —PRESIDENT HARRY S. TRUMAN

Jackie Robinson

1947

Jackie Robinson steps out onto the field for the Brooklyn Dodgers, breaking the color barrier in major-league baseball.

1947

In a speech at Harvard University, Secretary of State George C. Marshall, who was chief of staff of the U.S. Army in World War II, announces a plan for America to help Europe, which has been devastated by the war.

> *"The United States should do whatever it is able to do to assist in the return of normal economic health in the world, without which there can be no political stability and no assured peace. Our policy is directed not against any country or doctrine but against hunger, poverty, desperation, and chaos."*
>
> —George C. Marshall

THE MARSHALL PLAN, WHICH WAS CRUCIAL TO THE REBUILDING OF EUROPE, WAS OPPOSED BY THE SOVIET UNION, EVEN THOUGH THE USSR AND THE COUNTRIES IT DOMINATED WERE ELIGIBLE FOR AID. THE SOVIETS SUBSEQUENTLY PORTRAYED THE MARSHALL PLAN AS PART OF A U.S. ATTEMPT TO GAIN CONTROL OVER EUROPE.

"The soldier who saw his life's fulfillment in an act for peace . . . recruited us in the service of peace."

—WILLY BRANDT, chancellor of Germany, describing George C. Marshall on the twenty-fifth anniversary of the Marshall Plan's proposal

1947

Following a year in which millions of unionized workers have gone on strike, Congress passes the Taft-Hartley Act, curbing union power. When President Harry S. Truman vetoes it, Congress overrides his veto.

1947–48

At Bell Labs in New Jersey, John Bardeen, Walter Brattain, and William Shockley invent the transistor.

1948

Maj. Hector Garcia, a physician from Corpus Christi, Texas, founds the American GI Forum to address inequities experienced by Hispanic veterans.

IN THE YEARS SINCE ITS FOUNDING, THE AMERICAN GI FORUM HAS ALSO CALLED ATTENTION TO THE SERVICE OF HISPANICS IN THE U.S. ARMED FORCES. IN 2005 THE ORGANIZATION'S WEB SITE CARRIED THE story of Sgt. Rafael Peralta, who died in Fallujah, Iraq, shielding other marines from a grenade blast.

1948

Israel comes into being at midnight on May 14. Eleven minutes later the United States extends recognition.

1948

The Soviets, in control of the area of Germany around Berlin, cut off ground access to West Berlin, prompting Allied forces to begin airlifting food and supplies.

Meeting the needs of more than two million Berliners required British and American aircraft taking off and landing around the clock, sometimes as often as every ninety seconds. Airlift pilots ferried everything from food to seedling trees into the city, until on May 12, 1949, almost eleven months after the blockade had started, the Soviet Union discontinued it.

German children cheering an airlift plane

1948

At the Democratic convention in Philadelphia, thirty-five southern delegates walk out in protest over a civil rights plank in the party's platform.

> *"Segregation forever."*
>
> —Campaign slogan of the Dixiecrats, breakaway southern Democrats, who nominated South Carolina's Strom Thurmond for president

---

DEMOCRATIC LIBERALS WHO THOUGHT PRESIDENT HARRY S. TRUMAN'S FOREIGN POLICY TOO HARSH TOWARD THE SOVIET UNION FORMED YET ANOTHER PARTY. THEY NOMINATED HENRY WALLACE, WHO HAD BEEN FDR'S VICE PRESIDENT IMMEDIATELY BEFORE TRUMAN. PRESIDENT TRUMAN HAD FIRED WALLACE AS SECRETARY OF COMMERCE AFTER WALLACE PUBLICALLY CRITICIZED THE ADMINISTRATION'S "GET TOUGH" POLICY TOWARD THE USSR.

1948

President Truman issues Executive Order 9981, which provides for "equality of treatment and opportunity for all persons in the armed services without regard to race, color, religion or national origin."

> "BY EXECUTIVE ORDER—PRESIDENT TRUMAN WIPES OUT SEGREGATION IN ARMED FORCES."
>
> —*Chicago Defender* headline on July 31, 1948

1948

Faced with low poll numbers and a divided party, President Truman whistle-stops across the country, vigorously denouncing the Republican Congress. Defying almost every expert, he defeats Thomas Dewey.

President Harry S. Truman, celebrating his election

> "Dewey defeats Truman."
>
> —*Chicago Daily Tribune* headline, reporting the conventional wisdom before the votes were counted

1949

The Senate ratifies the treaty creating the North Atlantic Treaty Organization (NATO), an alliance that joins twelve countries—the United States, Canada, Belgium, Denmark, France, Iceland, Italy, Luxembourg, the Netherlands, Norway, Portugal, and the United Kingdom—in an agreement to treat an attack on any one of them as an attack on all of them. In 2005, NATO will have twenty-six members.

1949

News reaches the United States that the Soviets have successfully tested an atomic bomb.

SOVIET POSSESSION OF AN ATOMIC WEAPON LED PRESIDENT TRUMAN TO DECIDE TO SET THE UNITED STATES ON COURSE TO DEVELOP A HYDROGEN BOMB. HE MADE THIS DECISION OVER THE OBJECTIONS OF SOME ADVISING HIM, INCLUDING J. ROBERT OPPENHEIMER, LEADER OF THE TEAM THAT DESIGNED THE ATOMIC BOMB. THE SOVIETS TESTED AN H-BOMB IN 1953, A LITTLE MORE THAN NINE MONTHS AFTER THE AMERICANS.

1949

Forces under the leadership of Mao Tse-tung defeat the nationalist Chinese led by Chiang Kai-shek. China comes under Communist control.

1950

Alger Hiss, president of the Carnegie Endowment for International Peace and a former State Department official, is convicted of perjury.

WHITTAKER CHAMBERS, A FORMER COMMUNIST WHO HAD TURNED AWAY FROM THE PARTY, ACCUSED HISS OF BEING A COMMUNIST IN THE 1930S AND OF TURNING SECRET DOCUMENTS OVER TO THE SOVIETS. HISS, CONVICTED OF LYING IN HIS DENIALS OF CHAMBERS'S CHARGES, SERVED THREE YEARS OF A FIVE-YEAR PRISON SENTENCE.

1950

During a speech in Wheeling, West Virginia, Senator Joseph McCarthy of Wisconsin waves a piece of paper that he says contains the names of Communists in the State Department.

> "*I have here in my hand a list of 205 that were known to the secretary of state as being members of the Communist Party and who, nevertheless, are still working and shaping the policy in the State Department.*"
>
> —Senator Joseph McCarthy, as quoted in the *Wheeling Intelligencer*

The night after the Wheeling speech, McCarthy said that he had the names of "fifty-seven card-carrying members of the Communist Party." Eleven days later he talked about eighty-one cases of people with questionable loyalty.

1950

Eight North Korean divisions and an armored brigade, with 150 Soviet-made tanks in the lead, cross the thirty-eighth parallel and invade South Korea.

> "By God, *I am going to let them have it!*"
>
> —President Harry S. Truman

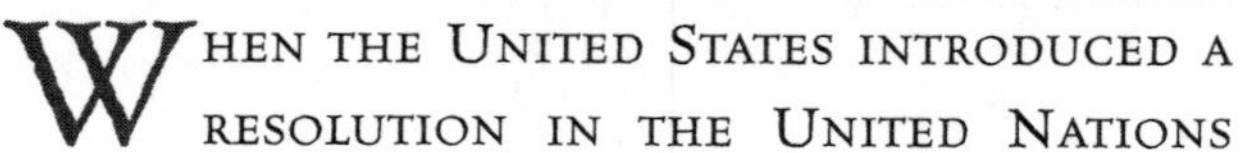
When the United States introduced a resolution in the United Nations

SECURITY COUNCIL CALLING FOR NORTH KOREA TO WITHDRAW FROM THE SOUTH, THE SOVIET UNION COULD NORMALLY HAVE BEEN COUNTED ON TO VETO SUCH A RESOLUTION. BUT THE SOVIETS WERE BOYCOTTING THE SECURITY COUNCIL BECAUSE IT WOULD NOT SEAT RED CHINA AND EXPEL THE NATIONALIST CHINESE. AND SO THE RESOLUTION WAS APPROVED.

1950

UN troops that are mostly American stop the North Korean advance only after the North Koreans have taken most of the peninsula. Gen. Douglas MacArthur lands troops at Inchon, behind enemy lines, and succeeds in driving North Korean forces to north of the thirty-eighth parallel. With President Truman's authorization MacArthur continues to advance toward the Yalu River, the boundary between North Korea and China.

1950

Two men, fanatic Puerto Rican nationalists, attempt to assassinate President Truman. They kill one, and wound two, of the men guarding the president.

ONE OF THE PUERTO RICANS WAS KILLED DURING THE ASSASSINATION ATTEMPT; THE OTHER WAS SENTENCED TO DEATH. SHORTLY BEFORE HE WAS TO BE EXECUTED, PRESIDENT TRUMAN COMMUTED HIS SENTENCE TO LIFE IN PRISON. PRESIDENT CARTER PARDONED HIM IN 1979.

1950

Chinese Communist troops attack in force, driving UN troops back until they are south of the thirty-eighth parallel. General MacArthur wants to take aggressive action against China, a course the president rejects.

1951

The Twenty-second Amendment to the Constitution is ratified. It provides that no president may serve more than two terms.

1951

After General MacArthur publically criticizes the Truman administration's policies, the president fires him.

Truman and MacArthur in happier times

Tens of thousands of people turned out to see MacArthur when he returned home to the United States. In an address to a joint session of Congress, he continued to advocate an aggressive approach to the Chinese.

"In war, indeed, there can be no substitute for victory."

—Gen. Douglas MacArthur

1952

His popularity ratings low, President Truman announces he will not run again. Dwight D. Eisenhower, who pledges to go to Korea and concentrate on ending the war, is elected president, the first Republican elected in twenty-four years. Seven months after his inauguration a truce is signed in Korea.

"I like Ike."

—Dwight "Ike" Eisenhower's campaign slogan

Eisenhower was the tenth general who had served in combat to be elected president. The others were George Washington, Andrew Jackson, William Henry Harrison, Zachary Taylor, Franklin Pierce, Ulysses S. Grant, Rutherford B. Hayes, James A. Garfield, and Benjamin Harrison.

Gen. Dwight D. Eisenhower on the campaign trail

1953

Julius and Ethel Rosenberg, convicted of passing information about America's atomic-weapons program to the Soviets during World War II, are executed. Their case will be passionately debated in the decades ahead.

Cables sent from Soviet missions in the United States to the Soviet intelligence service in Moscow during the 1940s were made public in 1995 and 1996. These communications, known as the Venona cables, confirm that Julius Rosenberg helped the USSR gain access to U.S. atomic secrets. Ethel Rosenberg was aware of what her husband was doing, but from what the Soviet documents show, she had a much less active role.

1953

Amid U.S. concerns that Iran will fall under Soviet influence, the Central Intelligence Agency helps bring about the downfall of premier Mohammad Mossadegh of Iran. Power is consolidated under the shah of Iran.

1954

The Army-McCarthy hearings, investigating accusations made by Senator Joseph McCarthy against the U.S. Army, and by the army against McCarthy, are televised.

Joseph McCarthy

> *"Have you no sense of decency, sir, at long last? Have you left no sense of decency?"*
>
> —Joseph Welch, army special counsel, to Senator McCarthy

By showing McCarthy's tactics of bullying and intimidation to millions of viewers,

THE HEARINGS HELPED BRING ABOUT HIS DOWNFALL. SIX MONTHS LATER THE SENATE CENSURED SENATOR MCCARTHY.

1954

In *Hernandez v. Texas* the U.S. Supreme Court rules that Mexican Americans are a discrete class when it comes to equal protection under the law and cannot be systematically excluded from juries.

1954

In *Brown v. Board of Education of Topeka*, the U.S. Supreme Court rules that "the 'separate but equal' doctrine adopted in *Plessy v. Ferguson* . . . has no place in the field of public education." The next year the Court will order schools desegregated.

MOTHER AND DAUGHTER AT U.S. SUPREME COURT THE DAY AFTER THE *BROWN V. BOARD OF EDUCATION* RULING

WHEN MOBS IN LITTLE ROCK, ARKANSAS, KEPT NINE BLACK STUDENTS FROM ATTENDING CENTRAL HIGH SCHOOL IN 1957, PRESIDENT

DWIGHT D. EISENHOWER SENT IN FEDERAL TROOPS. PRESIDENT JOHN F. KENNEDY DID THE SAME TO QUELL THE VIOLENCE THAT SURROUNDED JAMES MEREDITH'S ATTENDING THE UNIVERSITY OF MISSISSIPPI IN 1962.

1954

Fearing the spread of Communism, President Eisenhower approves plans to remove Guatemala's leader, Jacobo Arbenz Guzmán. He is replaced by Carlos Castillo Armas.

LATIN-AMERICAN RESENTMENT TOWARD THE UNITED STATES BECAME EVIDENT FOUR YEARS LATER WHEN VICE PRESIDENT RICHARD NIXON VISITED VENEZUELA AS PART OF A GOODWILL TOUR, AND A RIOTING MOB STONED HIS CAR.

1955

The Salk vaccine is found to be effective against polio, a disease that has killed or crippled tens of thousands of children.

Edward R. Murrow: "Who owns the patent on this vaccine?"

Dr. Jonas Salk: "Well, the people, I would say. There is no patent. Could you patent the sun?"

THE SALK VACCINE, WHICH USES A KILLED VIRUS, WAS THE PRIMARY PREVENTIVE AGAINST POLIO IN THE 1950S. IN THE 1960S THE LIVE-VIRUS VACCINE

DEVELOPED BY ALBERT SABIN BECAME PREDOMINANT. IN 2000 THE CENTERS FOR DISEASE CONTROL RECOMMENDED A RETURN TO THE SALK VACCINE.

ROSA PARKS

1955

In Montgomery, Alabama, Rosa Parks refuses to give up her seat on a bus to a white man and is arrested. African Americans boycott the city transportation for more than a year, returning only after a Supreme Court order desegregates the buses.

> *"The great glory of American democracy is the right to protest for right."*
>
> —MARTIN LUTHER KING JR., addressing a meeting in a Montgomery church

1956

President Dwight D. Eisenhower signs the Federal Highway Act, transforming travel by automobile.

THE ACT CREATED AN INTERSTATE SYSTEM THAT EVENTUALLY COMPRISED MORE THAN FORTY THOUSAND MILES OF DIVIDED, TWO-LANE HIGHWAYS FREE OF INTERSECTIONS, TRAFFIC SIGNALS, AND RAILROAD CROSSINGS. THE SYSTEM LATER BYPASSED TOWNS AND EVEN LEGENDARY HIGHWAYS LIKE ROUTE 66, IMMORTALIZED IN JOHN STEINBECK'S *THE GRAPES OF WRATH* AS "THE MOTHER ROAD."

1956

President Eisenhower is reelected.

1957

The nation is stunned when the Soviet Union successfully places an unmanned satellite in space. It is known as *Sputnik*, which means "fellow traveler."

THE UNITED STATES SPEEDED UP ITS EFFORTS TO GET ITS OWN SATELLITE INTO ORBIT, TO UNFORTUNATE END AT FIRST. IN DECEMBER 1957 THE ROCKET CARRYING THE U.S. SATELLITE ROSE THREE FEET OFF ITS LAUNCH PAD—AND TOPPLED OVER IN FLAMES. NEWSPAPERS CALLED IT "KAPUTNIK," "FLOPNIK," AND "STAYPUTNIK." THE NEXT MONTH THE UNITED STATES SUCCESSFULLY LAUNCHED *EXPLORER I*.

1958–59

Working separately, Jack Kilby and Robert Noyce each invent the integrated circuit.

> *"Integrated circuits will lead to such wonders as home computers—or at least terminals connected to a central computer—automatic controls for automobiles, and personal portable communications equipment. The electronic wristwatch needs only a display to be feasible today."*
>
> —Gordon E. Moore, future cofounder of Intel Corporation, in 1965

1959

Alaska joins the Union as the forty-ninth state.

1959

Fidel Castro seizes power in Cuba. Over the next months concerns will grow that he is allying himself with the Soviet Union.

In the decades after Castro's takeover in Cuba, hundreds of thousands of Cubans fled to the United States.

1959

Vice President Richard Nixon, on a trip to the Soviet Union, debates the merits of capitalism versus Communism with Soviet premier Nikita Khrushchev as the two men tour a model American kitchen at a Moscow trade fair.

"This is what America is capable of, and how long has she existed? Three hundred years? One hundred fifty years of independence and this is her level. We haven't quite reached forty-two years, and in another seven years, we'll be at the level of America, and after that we'll go farther. As we pass you by, we'll wave 'hi' to you."

—Nikita Khrushchev, to Richard Nixon

Vice President Richard Nixon making a point to Soviet premier Nikita Khrushchev

1959

Hawaii joins the Union as the fiftieth state.

1960

Four students from North Carolina Agricultural and Technical College take seats at a segregated lunch counter in Greensboro, starting a movement that will sweep across the South.

1960

The Soviets shoot down a U-2 spy plane flying over the USSR.

1960

The birth control pill is introduced. Within five years five million women will be using it.

1960

Senator John F. Kennedy, a Democrat from Massachusetts, defeats Dwight D. Eisenhower's vice president, Richard Nixon, for the presidency of the United States.

> "*Let every nation know, whether it wishes us well or ill, that we shall pay any price, bear any burden, meet any hardship, support any friend, oppose any foe, in order to assure the survival and the success of liberty.*"
>
> —PRESIDENT JOHN F. KENNEDY, in his inaugural address

1961

Signing an executive order, President Kennedy creates the Peace Corps, an organization that provides volunteer help for interested countries and aims at fostering mutual understanding.

THE 1960S WERE A TIME OF YOUTHFUL IDEALISM, AS THE PEACE CORPS RECOGNIZED. YOUNG PEOPLE ALSO BEGAN DIRECTING THEIR HOPES FOR A BETTER WORLD TOWARD POLITICS.

> "*We, as young conservatives, believe: . . . That we will be free only so long as the national sovereignty of the United States is secure; that history shows periods of freedom are rare, and can exist only when free citizens concertedly defend their rights against*

all enemies; That the forces of international Communism are, at present, the greatest single threat to these liberties."

—Founding statement of Young Americans for Freedom, 1960

"An unreasoning anticommunism has become a major social problem for those who want to construct a more democratic America. . . . Disarmament should be continually avowed as a national goal."

—Port Huron Statement, Students for a Democratic Society, 1962

1961

President Kennedy approves a covert operation to land Cuban exiles in Cuba and overthrow Fidel Castro. The invasion at the Bay of Pigs is a debacle, and nearly twelve thousand exiles are taken prisoner.

A SECRET PROGRAM KNOWN AS OPERATION MONGOOSE WAS SET UP AFTER THE BAY OF PIGS INVASION TO BRING DOWN THE CASTRO REGIME. PLANS WERE MADE FOR DESTABILIZING THE COUNTRY AND EVEN ASSASSINATING THE CUBAN LEADER.

1961

With Soviet approval a wall is erected in Berlin to prevent those living in the East, the Soviet-controlled part of the city, from escaping to the West. Over the next twenty-eight years more than two hundred will die trying to cross the wall.

IN 1962 PETER FECHTER, AN EIGHTEEN-YEAR-OLD BRICKLAYER, TRIED TO ESCAPE THE EAST BY CLIMBING THE WALL. SHOT IN THE BACK, HE FELL INTO THE NO-MAN'S-LAND BETWEEN EAST AND WEST AND BLED TO DEATH IN VIEW OF AN OUTRAGED BUT HELPLESS CROWD. BERLINERS RIOTED, BUT THE WALL REMAINED.

TO INDICATE SOLIDARITY WITH THE PEOPLE OF BERLIN, PRESIDENT KENNEDY VISITED THE CITY IN 1963.

> "*All free men, wherever they may live, are citizens of* Berlin, *and, therefore, as a free man,* I *take pride in the words* 'Ich bin ein Berliner.'"
>
> —President John F. Kennedy

1962

When U.S. aerial reconnaissance spots Soviet missiles in Cuba, President Kennedy imposes a blockade. Soviet freighters headed toward the island turn back, and the Soviets remove their missiles.

President John F. Kennedy and his brother Attorney General Robert F. Kennedy at the White House

It was later learned that President Kennedy agreed to take U.S. missiles out of Turkey in exchange for the Soviets' removing their missiles from Cuba.

1963

Authorities in Birmingham, Alabama, use fire hoses and dogs against civil rights demonstrators, including children. President Kennedy proposes civil rights legislation.

1963

Medgar Evers, first field secretary for the NAACP in Mississippi, is murdered by a white supremacist.

"Freedom has never been free. . . . I love my children and I love my wife with all my heart. And I would die, and die gladly, if that would make a better life for them."

—Medgar Evers

1963

To encourage congressional action on a civil rights bill, 250,000 people march on Washington, D.C.

Martin Luther King Jr., at the March on Washington

"I have a dream that my four little children will one day live in a nation where they will not be judged by the color of their skin but by the content of their character."

—Martin Luther King Jr., speaking at the Lincoln Memorial

1963

In Vietnam—where the Communist North Vietnamese, under Ho Chi Minh, are at war with the South

Vietnamese, led by Ngo Dinh Diem—President John F. Kennedy expands American military support of the south to some sixteen thousand advisers. Believing Diem to be an inept leader, President Kennedy supports a secret effort to replace him. Diem is overthrown and killed.

AMERICA WAS IN VIETNAM BECAUSE OF A CONCERN EXPRESSED BY PRESIDENT DWIGHT D. EISENHOWER IN 1954 AND SHARED BY PRESIDENT KENNEDY: A COMMUNIST TAKEOVER OF THE SOUTH WOULD CAUSE OTHER COUNTRIES TO FALL TO THE COMMUNISTS AND THUS ULTIMATELY ENDANGER THE UNITED STATES.

"You have a row of dominoes set up, you knock over the first one, and what will happen to the last one is the certainty that it will go over very quickly. So you could have a beginning of a disintegration that would have the most profound influences."

—President Dwight D. Eisenhower

1963

On a trip to Dallas, Texas, on November 22, President Kennedy is assassinated.

PRESIDENT KENNEDY'S ASSASSIN, LEE HARVEY OSWALD, WAS ASSASSINATED HIMSELF TWO DAYS LATER BY A MAN NAMED JACK RUBY. THE WARREN COMMISSION, APPOINTED BY PRESIDENT LYNDON B. JOHNSON, CONCLUDED THAT BOTH OSWALD AND RUBY ACTED ALONE, BUT CONSPIRACY THEORISTS EVER SINCE HAVE TRIED TO PROVE OTHERWISE.

Don't let it be forgot
That once there was a spot
For one brief shining moment
That was known as Camelot.

—Alan Jay Lerner, "Camelot." A few days after the president's death, Mrs. Kennedy said her husband had especially loved this song.

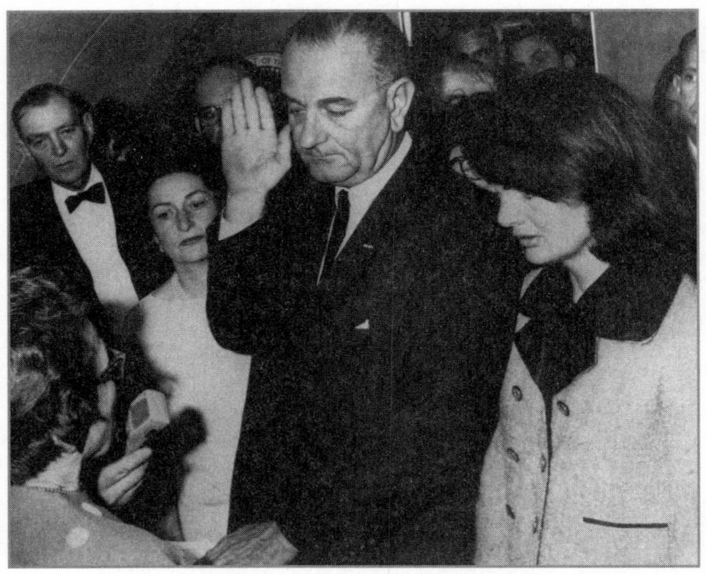

Lyndon Johnson taking the presidential oath

1964

In his first State of the Union message, President Lyndon B. Johnson announces his intention to fight a war on poverty. Among the programs that will be created are the Job Corps and Head Start.

1964

Congress passes historic tax cuts, and President Johnson signs them into law.

These reductions are commonly referred to as the Kennedy tax cuts because they were proposed by President John F. Kennedy on January 24, 1963.

1964

In *New York Times v. Sullivan,* the U.S. Supreme Court rules that in order for a public figure to win a libel case, he or she must prove "actual malice": that is, that a damaging statement has been made "with knowledge that it was false or with reckless disregard of whether it was false or not."

According to Justice William Brennan, writing for the Court, debate on public issues should be able to include "vehement, caustic, and sometimes unpleasantly sharp attacks on government and public officials." The country had come a long way since John Adams put his critics in jail.

1964

Andrew Goodman, James Chaney, and Michael Schwerner, working to register black voters in Mississippi as part of "Freedom Summer," are murdered by a mob dominated by Ku Klux Klansmen.

1964

Congress passes, and President Lyndon B. Johnson signs, the Civil Rights Act of 1964. It outlaws employment discrimination on the basis of race, color, religion, sex, or national origin and prohibits racial discrimination in places of public accommodation.

The civil rights bill passed as a result of bipartisan effort. In the House of Representatives 152 of the 248 Democrats who voted on the bill supported it, as did 138 of the 172 Republicans. In the Senate, where 18 southern Democrats and 1 southern Republican filibustered, 44 Democrats (out of a total of 67) and 27 Republicans (of a total of 33) succeeded in bringing cloture—that is, ending the filibuster.

> *"Stronger than all the armies is an idea whose time has come."*
>
> —Senate minority leader Everett Dirksen, paraphrasing Victor Hugo, as he worked to pass the Civil Rights Act

1964

The Republicans nominate Barry Goldwater as their candidate for president.

> *"Extremism in the defense of liberty is no vice. And . . . moderation in the pursuit of justice is no virtue."*
>
> —Senator Barry Goldwater

1964

Seizing upon reports of an August 4 attack on American destroyers off Vietnam in the Tonkin Gulf, President Lyndon B. Johnson asks Congress to support action to deal with such aggression. In the Gulf of Tonkin Resolution, Congress

authorizes the president to take "all necessary measures" to repel future attacks and "to prevent further aggression."

FIRE WAS EXCHANGED BETWEEN NORTH VIETNAMESE PATROL BOATS AND THE USS *MADDOX* ON AUGUST 2 WHILE THE *MADDOX* WAS ON A RECONNAISSANCE MISSION IN THE GULF. THE AUGUST 4 ATTACK MAY NOT HAVE OCCURRED. MISINTERPRETED SONAR SIGNALS MAY HAVE MISLED SAILORS ON TWO SHIPS IN THE GULF INTO THINKING THEY HAD BEEN ATTACKED.

1965

After defeating Goldwater, President Johnson calls in his State of the Union message for America to become a "Great Society." Among the programs that the Great Society will encompass are Medicare, Medicaid, and the Voting Rights Act of 1965.

PRESIDENT JOHNSON CALLED FOR PASSAGE OF THE VOTING RIGHTS ACT ON MARCH 15, ONE WEEK AND ONE DAY AFTER VOTING-RIGHTS DEMONSTRATORS ATTEMPTING TO MARCH FROM SELMA, ALABAMA, TO MONTGOMERY WERE CLUBBED AND TEARGASSED.

We shall overcome, we shall overcome,
We shall overcome some day
Oh, deep in my heart I do believe
We shall overcome some day.

—The song sung by marchers as they made their way from Selma to Montgomery. It was an anthem of the civil rights movement.

1965

President Johnson orders air raids on North Vietnam. He will also increase draft calls, which in 1966 will reach 400,000. In 1968 there will be 537,800 troops in Vietnam.

> "*I have asked the commanding general, General Westmoreland, what more he needs to meet this mounting aggression. He has told me. We will meet his needs. . . . We will stand in Vietnam.*"
>
> —President Lyndon B. Johnson

Marines landing at Da Nang, Vietnam

1965

President Johnson orders a bombing pause, as he repeatedly will, hoping to bring the North Vietnamese to the negotiating table. They do not respond.

1965

African Americans burn Watts, a neighborhood in Los Angeles. The next few years will see race riots in dozens of cities, including Chicago, Detroit, and Washington, D.C.

"Burn, baby, burn!"

—Rioters in Watts

1965

César Chávez leads the National Farm Workers Association in a strike against grape growers. In a lifetime of labor activism, he will stress nonviolence as a way to achieve rights for farmworkers.

César Chávez

1965

At President Johnson's urging, Congress passes the Immigration and Nationality Act, which does away with quotas based on national origin. Many new immigrants will come from Asia and Latin America.

1965

In the Ia Drang Valley troopers of the First Cavalry Division defeat three North Vietnamese regiments, killing nearly two thousand of the enemy but sustaining terrible losses of their own. More than three hundred Americans die in the operation.

1967

President Johnson nominates Thurgood Marshall to the U.S. Supreme Court. He becomes the first African-American justice.

1967

Antiwar demonstrators mass at the Lincoln Memorial in Washington, D.C. After peaceful protests and a moment of silence for Cuban revolutionary Che Guevara, about 35,000 march to the Pentagon, where some try to storm the building.

1967

Minnesota senator Eugene McCarthy, a Democrat, announces he is running for president as an antiwar candidate.

THOUSANDS OF ANTIWAR STUDENTS WORKED IN THE MCCARTHY CAMPAIGN, MANY OF THEM GOING "CLEAN FOR GENE"—CUTTING OFF THEIR HAIR AND SHAVING THEIR BEARDS.

1967

The number of Americans killed in Vietnam during this year is 11,153. By the end of the war, more than 58,000 will have died.

1968

Vietcong (Communist guerrillas) and North Vietnamese regulars launch an offensive on the first day of Tet, a holiday celebrating the lunar New Year. They raid dozens of cities and hamlets, only to be repulsed, and lose as many as fifty thousand men.

THE TET OFFENSIVE WAS A VICTORY FOR THE SOUTH BUT WAS NOT GENERALLY PERCEIVED THAT WAY IN THE UNITED STATES. TELEVISION IMAGES OF VIETCONG BREACHING THE WALLS OF THE U.S. EMBASSY IN SAIGON WERE VERY POWERFUL, AND IN THE WEEKS FOLLOWING, OPINION LEADERS SPOKE OUT AGAINST THE WAR.

> "*It seems now more certain than ever that the bloody experience of* Vietnam *is to end in a stalemate.*"
>
> —CBS anchor WALTER CRONKITE

1968

After Eugene McCarthy comes close to beating him in the New Hampshire primary, President Lyndon B. Johnson announces he will not be a candidate for reelection.

> "I *shall not seek, and* I *will not accept, the nomination of my party for another term as your president.*"
>
> —PRESIDENT LYNDON B. JOHNSON

1968

Martin Luther King Jr. is assassinated by James Earl Ray in Memphis, Tennessee.

> "I *just want to do* God's *will.* And He's *allowed me to go up to the mountain.* And I've *looked over.* And I've *seen the promised land.* I *may not get there with you.* But I *want you to know tonight, that we, as a people, will get to the promised land.* And I'm *happy,*

tonight. I'm not worried about anything. I'm not fearing any man. Mine eyes have seen the glory of the coming of the Lord."

—Martin Luther King Jr., the night before he was killed

1968

Senator Robert F. Kennedy, campaigning for the Democratic presidential nomination, wins the California primary and is assassinated by Sirhan Sirhan, a fanatic Arab nationalist, in Los Angeles.

"Some men see things as they are and say 'Why?' I dream things that never were and say 'Why not?'"

—Robert F. Kennedy, paraphrasing a favorite quotation from George Bernard Shaw

1968

Police use clubs and tear gas against antiwar demonstrators at the Democratic convention in Chicago. Vice President Hubert Humphrey is nominated to be the Democratic candidate for president of the United States.

1968

Women protest the Miss America Pageant in Atlantic City as oppressive and demeaning to women. They throw bras and girdles into a trash can.

What is sometimes called the second wave of feminism had been building since at least 1963, when Betty Friedan published *The Feminine Mystique*. Women had organized to demand their rights, forming the National Organization for Women in 1966.

"Real power to control our own lives is restricted to men, while women get patronizing pseudo-power, an ermine cloak and a bunch of flowers; men are judged by their actions, women by appearance."

—From "No More Miss America!," an announcement of the protest

1968

Richard Nixon, a Republican, is elected president.

1969

Astronaut Neil Armstrong walks on the moon.

Neil Armstrong on the moon

"That's one small step for a man, one giant leap for mankind."

—Neil Armstrong

1969

President Richard Nixon undertakes "Vietnamization"—shifting responsibility to the South Vietnamese—and begins troop withdrawals to shrink American forces in Vietnam. The Defense Department reduces draft calls.

IN NOVEMBER BETWEEN 250,000 AND 500,000 CONVERGED ON WASHINGTON IN THE LARGEST ANTIWAR PROTEST IN U.S. HISTORY. BUSES WERE LINED UP END TO END AROUND THE WHITE HOUSE TO PROTECT IT. ARMED TROOPS GUARDED LANDMARKS.

1969

With the sponsorship of the Defense Department's Advanced Research Projects Agency (ARPA), scientists connect computers at the University of California–Los Angeles, Stanford Research Institute, the University of California–Santa Barbara, and the University of Utah, creating ARPANET, and the Internet begins.

1970

President Nixon announces the Cambodian incursion, American troops attacking Vietcong and North Vietnamese bases in Cambodia.

THE SENDING OF AMERICAN TROOPS INTO CAMBODIA SPARKED CAMPUS PROTESTS. AT KENT STATE UNIVERSITY IN OHIO, NATIONAL GUARDSMEN FIRED INTO A CROWD AND KILLED FOUR, SETTING OFF STILL MORE PROTESTS ON CAMPUSES ACROSS THE NATION. STUDENT STRIKES SHUT DOWN HUNDREDS OF UNIVERSITIES.

1970

President Nixon signs a bill creating the Environmental Protection Agency.

1970–71

Federico Faggin, Ted Hoff, and Stanley Mazor invent the microprocessor, a central processing unit on a single chip that will become the heart of almost all computers.

1971

A secret study of U.S. involvement in Vietnam, the "Pentagon Papers," is leaked to the *New York Times* by Daniel Ellsberg. The administration seeks an injunction to halt publication, but the Supreme Court rules that it can proceed.

1972

His way paved by national security adviser Henry Kissinger, President Nixon makes a historic visit to China, then three months later goes to Moscow.

PRESIDENT NIXON AT GREAT WALL OF CHINA

THE POLICY THAT LED TO PRESIDENT NIXON'S VISITS IS CALLED DÉTENTE, WHICH IS A RELAXING OF TENSIONS BETWEEN COUNTRIES. SINCE THE PRESIDENT WAS KNOWN AS A DEDICATED ANTICOMMUNIST,

HE WAS ABLE TO TRAVEL TO CHINA AND THE USSR WITHOUT SEEMING TO BE WEAK ON COMMUNISM.

1972

Congress passes the Equal Rights Amendment and sends it to the states to be ratified.

> *"Equality of rights under the law shall not be denied or abridged by the United States or by any state on account of sex."*
>
> —Equal Rights Amendment, Section 1

WITHIN A YEAR THIRTY STATES HAD APPROVED THE ERA, BUT IN THE END IT WAS NOT RATIFIED, LARGELY OWING TO THE EFFORTS OF PHYLLIS SCHLAFLY, WHO ORGANIZED STOP ERA. MEMBERS OF THIS MOVEMENT VIEWED THE AMENDMENT AS THREATENING WOMEN'S TRADITIONAL ROLE AND GIVING TOO MUCH POWER OVER FAMILY LIFE TO THE FEDERAL GOVERNMENT.

1972

Five men are arrested for breaking into the Watergate offices of the Democratic National Committee.

> "A *third-rate burglary attempt.*"
>
> —White House spokesman RONALD ZIEGLER's description

1972

President Richard Nixon signs Title IX of the Education Amendments Act of 1972. It prohibits excluding individuals on the basis of sex from programs or activities at educational institutions receiving federal funds.

TITLE IX RESULTED IN A DRAMATIC INCREASE IN SPORTS PROGRAMS FOR WOMEN AND A NEW ERA IN WOMEN'S ATHLETIC ACCOMPLISHMENT.

1972

Campaigning on a platform of "peace with honor," President Nixon is reelected, beating his opponent, Senator George McGovern, in every state except Massachusetts.

1972

The last draftee receives his induction notice. Following on a campaign promise that President Nixon made in 1968 and has worked to implement since, the all-volunteer army will begin the next year.

1973

In *Roe v. Wade* the U.S. Supreme Court invalidates many state abortion laws, ruling that in the first trimester abortion decisions must be left to doctors. After that, up to the point of viability, the state may regulate abortion procedures to protect maternal health.

> *"For the stage subsequent to viability, the state, in promoting its interest in the potentiality of human life, may, if it chooses, regulate, and even proscribe,*

abortion except where it is necessary, in appropriate medical judgment, for the preservation of the life or health of the mother."

—Justice Harry A. Blackmun, delivering the opinion of the Court

1973

With Paris peace talks in their fifth year, the United States, North Vietnam, the Vietcong, and South Vietnam sign an accord. American prisoners of war begin coming home. American forces are withdrawn from Vietnam.

"*We have told* Hanoi, *privately and publicly, that we will not tolerate violations of the agreement.*"

—President Richard Nixon

1973

A defendant in the Watergate break-in claims that he and others were pressured to plead guilty and remain silent during their trial, that perjury occurred, and that others not identified during the trial were involved.

1973

To block any U.S. response to Communist violations of the Paris Peace Accords, Congress votes to deny further funding for military activities in Vietnam, Cambodia, or Laos.

1973

Testimony before the Senate Watergate committee reveals that the president has secretly taped conversations in the Oval Office.

1973

Accused of accepting bribes, Vice President Spiro Agnew pleads no contest to tax evasion and resigns from office.

Congressman Gerald R. Ford of Michigan will become vice president.

THE APPOINTMENT OF FORD AS VICE PRESIDENT WAS MADE POSSIBLE BY THE TWENTY-FIFTH AMENDMENT, RATIFIED IN 1967. BEFORE THAT TIME VACANCIES IN THE VICE PRESIDENCY REMAINED UNTIL THE NEXT ELECTION. WHILE LYNDON B. JOHNSON WAS SERVING OUT THE REMAINDER OF JOHN F. KENNEDY'S TERM, FOR EXAMPLE, HE HAD NO VICE PRESIDENT.

1973

After the United States supports Israel in the Yom Kippur War, the Organization of Petroleum Exporting Countries (OPEC) imposes an oil embargo. Oil prices quadruple and gas lines grow.

BETWEEN THE TIME THE EMBARGO WAS IMPOSED IN OCTOBER 1973 AND THE TIME IT WAS LIFTED IN MARCH 1974, CONGRESS APPROVED THE BUILDING OF THE 800-MILE TRANS-ALASKA PIPELINE TO CARRY OIL FROM PRUDHOE BAY TO THE PORT OF VALDEZ.

1974

The Supreme Court rules that the president must turn over tapes he has been withholding to the Watergate special prosecutor. The House Judiciary Committee adopts articles of impeachment that charge the president with obstructing justice and misusing the powers of his office.

1974

The last of the withheld tapes are made public, and it becomes evident that not only will the House vote to impeach the president, the Senate is likely to convict him. President Richard Nixon resigns, and Gerald R. Ford becomes president of the United States.

> *"My fellow Americans, our long national nightmare is over. Our Constitution works; our great Republic is a government of laws and not of men. Here the people rule."*
>
> —President Gerald R. Ford

1974

President Ford pardons former president Nixon.

President Ford's decision was an unpopular one at the time. Twenty-seven years later, at the John F. Kennedy Library, he received a Profile in Courage Award for it.

> *"As president, he made a controversial decision of conscience to . . . end the national trauma of Watergate. In doing so, he placed his love of country ahead of his own political future."*
>
> —Caroline Kennedy

President Ford signing Richard Nixon's pardon

1974

Democrats prevail in congressional elections. Seventy-five new Democratic members, called "Watergate babies," are elected to the House of Representatives.

1975

The Indian Self-Determination and Education Assistance Act, promoting Indian self-governance, becomes law.

1975

President Ford requests military and economic aid for Vietnam, as well as Cambodia, which is under threat from the Khmer Rouge, a Communist movement. Congress refuses.

1975

North Vietnamese forces launch a major offensive, the South Vietnamese retreat, and Saigon falls. In the frantic hours before the end, hundreds of Americans and thousands of South Vietnamese are evacuated.

When South Vietnam fell, hundreds of thousands of South Vietnamese fled, many taking to the open sea in small boats. After spending time in refugee camps, many of these Vietnamese settled in the United States.

In Cambodia, which fell shortly before South Vietnam, the Khmer Rouge claimed the lives of more than a million people.

1975

In Finland, President Gerald R. Ford signs the Helsinki Accords, which commit thirty-five nations, including the Soviet Union, to respect "freedom of thought, conscience, religion or belief, for all."

> "*It is important that you recognize the deep devotion of the American people and their government to human rights and fundamental freedoms and thus to the pledges that this conference has made regarding the freer movement of people, ideas, information.*"
>
> —President Gerald R. Ford, addressing all of the Helsinki delegates, but in particular, Soviet leader Leonid Brezhnev

Following the Helsinki accords various organizations, such as Moscow Helsinki Group, began monitoring whether or not the Soviet Union was living up to the agreement.

THESE ORGANIZATIONS KEPT THE WORLD'S ATTENTION FOCUSED ON HUMAN RIGHTS VIOLATIONS, INCLUDING THE BANISHMENT OF ANDREI SAKHAROV AND THE IMPRISONMENT OF YURI ORLOV, NATAN SHARANSKY, AND SERGEI KOVALEV.

1975

In early September a woman points a gun at President Ford and is grabbed by a Secret Service agent. Later in the month another woman fires a shot at him and misses.

1976

Former Georgia governor Jimmy Carter defeats President Ford.

> *"I'll never lie to you."*
>
> —JIMMY CARTER, campaigning for president

1977

President Carter signs a treaty providing for the gradual transfer of the Panama Canal to the Panamanians. The Senate will ratify the treaty by a single vote.

ON DECEMBER 31, 1999, SOVEREIGNTY OVER THE PANAMA CANAL PASSED TO PANAMA.

1978

The U.S. Supreme Court rules in favor of Allan Bakke, who claims to be a victim of reverse discrimination. He was denied admission to the University of California–Davis medical school although his grades were higher than successful minority applicants'.

Four justices agreed that Bakke had been discriminated against. Four others said that the university had the right to use race as a factor in making admissions. Justice Lewis Powell voted with both groups, with the result that Bakke was admitted and the UC–Davis quota system was overturned, but the principle of affirmative action was upheld.

1978

At President Carter's invitation, Egyptian president Anwar Sadat and Israeli prime minister Menachem Begin come to Camp David, the presidential retreat in Maryland, for peace talks. The agreements they arrive at, the Camp David Accords, become the basis for a 1979 peace treaty between Egypt and Israel.

Egyptian president Anwar Sadat, President Carter, and Israeli prime minister Menachem Begin at the signing of the Camp David accords

THE MEETINGS AT CAMP DAVID LASTED THIRTEEN DAYS. AT ONE POINT PRESIDENT CARTER TOOK HIS GUESTS TO THE NEARBY GETTYSBURG BATTLEFIELD FOR A BREAK AND AS A REMINDER OF THE NEED FOR PEACE. SADAT KNEW MANY DETAILS OF THE BATTLE. BEGIN RECITED THE GETTYSBURG ADDRESS.

1979

An accident at the Three Mile Island nuclear power station near Harrisburg, Pennsylvania, leads to a partial meltdown of the core in the number two reactor and a release of radioactive gases.

THE AMOUNT OF RADIATION RELEASED WAS MINIMAL, AND, ACCORDING TO THE NUCLEAR REGULATORY COMMISSION, COMPREHENSIVE STUDIES SINCE THE ACCIDENT HAVE CONCLUDED THAT HEALTH EFFECTS WERE NEGLIGIBLE. BUT THREE MILE ISLAND CALLED INTO QUESTION THE FUTURE OF NUCLEAR ENERGY IN THE UNITED STATES.

1979

After OPEC announces price increases, gas lines grow and gas prices skyrocket in the United States. President Carter's approval rating plummets, and he retreats to Camp David for more than a week. Then he speaks to the American people.

> "I *want to talk to you right now about a fundamental threat to American democracy. . . . It is a crisis of confidence. It is a crisis that strikes at the*

very heart and soul and spirit of our national will. We can see this crisis in the growing doubt about the meaning of our own lives and in the loss of a unity of purpose for our nation."

—President Jimmy Carter

This speech has come to be known as the malaise speech, though in fact that word does not appear in it.

In 1980 the "Misery Index," which is unemployment plus inflation, reached 21 percent, a height not reached since the Great Depression and never exceeded since.

1979

After the shah of Iran falls from power, Iranian students seize hostages at the American embassy in Tehran.

Flag burning at U.S. embassy in Iran

A 1980 MISSION TO RESCUE AMERICAN HOSTAGES ENCOUNTERED A SANDSTORM THAT FORCED TWO HELICOPTERS TO TURN BACK. AT DESERT ONE, A SITE IN IRAN, THERE WAS A COLLISION BETWEEN A HELICOPTER AND A C-130 AIRCRAFT THAT KILLED EIGHT AMERICANS. THE MISSION WAS ABORTED.

1980

Former California governor Ronald Reagan, a Republican, defeats President Carter.

> *"Are you better off now than you were four years ago?"*
>
> —RONALD REAGAN, campaigning for president

1981

President Reagan is inaugurated. The Iranian government releases fifty-two American hostages.

PRESIDENT RONALD REAGAN

1981

A little more than two months after he is sworn into office, President Reagan is shot by John Hinckley Jr. The wound is serious, but he recovers quickly, and his sense of humor reassures the nation.

> "Honey, I *forgot to duck*."
>
> —President Ronald Reagan, to his wife, Nancy, borrowing a line from Jack Dempsey

---

President Reagan liked funny quotes, but also inspiring ones: Franklin D. Roosevelt's "This generation of Americans has a rendezvous with destiny"; Abraham Lincoln's description of America as the "last, best hope of earth"; Thomas Paine's declaration, "We have it in our power to begin the world over again"; and John Winthrop's hope that "we shall be as a city upon a hill."

1981

At the president's urging, Congress passes non–defense budget cuts and a historic tax reduction. The economy is slow to improve, but by 1983 the recession will be over and a period of prosperity will begin.

> "*Those same critics aren't calling it* Reaganomics *anymore*."
>
> —President Ronald Reagan, speaking in 1986

AT THE SAME TIME THAT HE WAS PROPOSING NON–DEFENSE BUDGET CUTS, PRESIDENT REAGAN WAS ADVOCATING SIGNIFICANT INCREASES IN MILITARY SPENDING. HE OVERSAW THE BIGGEST PEACETIME DEFENSE BUILDUP IN AMERICA'S HISTORY.

1981

President Reagan nominates Sandra Day O'Connor to the U.S. Supreme Court. She becomes the first female justice.

1981

IBM announces the IBM personal computer. PCs will come to dominate the computer industry.

1982

The computer is *Time* magazine's Man of the Year.

> *"There are some occasions . . . when the most significant force in a year's news is not a single individual but a process, and a widespread recognition by a whole society that this process is changing the course of all other processes."*
>
> —*Time* magazine

1983

President Reagan gives a speech in which he describes the Soviet Union as "an evil empire."

> "I *believe that Communism is another sad, bizarre chapter in human history whose last pages even now are being written."*
>
> —PRESIDENT RONALD REAGAN

1983

As part of his effort to build America's military strength, President Reagan proposes the Strategic Defense Initiative (SDI). Its goal is a technology to intercept and destroy missiles before they reach their targets.

> "*I call upon the scientific community in our country, those who gave us nuclear weapons, to turn their great talents now to the cause of mankind and world peace, to give us the means of rendering these nuclear weapons impotent and obsolete.*"
>
> —President Ronald Reagan

THE UNITED STATES MILITARY BUILDUP WAS BRINGING PRESSURE ON A SOVIET UNION WITH AN INCREASINGLY TROUBLED ECONOMY. THE USSR ALSO HAD PROBLEMS IN POLAND, WHERE SOLIDARITY, A LABOR MOVEMENT, PERSISTED DESPITE THE EFFORTS OF THE SOVIET-BACKED GOVERNMENT TO REPRESS IT. BY THE END OF THE DECADE, SOLIDARITY CANDIDATES WERE RUNNING FOR OFFICE.

> "*I am a son of this nation and that is why I feel profoundly all its noble aspirations, its desire to live in truth, liberty, justice and social solidarity, its desire to live its own life.*"
>
> —Pope John Paul II, speaking in Poland in 1983, offering hope, as he did repeatedly, to Polish people struggling to be free

1983

Part of a peacekeeping force, 241 service members, most of them U.S. Marines, are killed when a terrorist explodes a truck bomb at their barracks in Beirut, Lebanon. Within six months the remaining marines will be removed.

1983

When a hard-line Marxist military government comes to power on the island of Grenada through a bloody coup, the United States sends in forces to rescue Americans and remove the pro-Castro regime.

1984

President Ronald Reagan and his vice president, George H. W. Bush, seek reelection, running against former vice president Walter Mondale and New York congresswoman Geraldine Ferraro, the first woman to run on a major party's national ticket.

> "I *will not make age an issue of this campaign.* I *am not going to exploit, for political purposes, my opponent's youth and inexperience.*"
>
> —PRESIDENT RONALD REAGAN, the oldest president in U.S. history, in his second debate with Walter Mondale

1985

In his State of the Union speech, the president declares support for freedom fighters "on every continent, from Afghanistan to Nicaragua."

"Freedom is not the sole prerogative of a chosen few; it is the universal right of all God's children."

—President Ronald Reagan

1986

America celebrates the first annual national holiday commemorating Martin Luther King Jr.

1986

President Reagan and Mikhail Gorbachev, the general secretary of the Communist Party and leader of the Soviet Union, meet in Reykjavík, Iceland. This summit, like a previous one in Geneva, Switzerland, produces little result because of Soviet insistence that President Reagan abandon SDI.

Secretary Gorbachev, who advocated glasnost (openness) as well as perestroika (restructuring), was a new kind of Soviet leader, but he faced old problems, including a Soviet economy made dysfunctional in part by a defense budget that was one quarter of the country's gross national product.

1986

President Reagan, who has authorized the sale of missiles to Iran in exchange for Iranian help with freeing Americans held hostage in Lebanon, denies that he traded arms for hostages. He will later make a clarification.

"A few months ago I told the American people I did not trade arms for hostages. My heart and my best

intentions still tell me that's true, but the facts and the evidence tell me it is not."

—President Ronald Reagan, on his involvement in the arms-for-hostages matter

Money from the sale of weapons to Iran was sent to the Contras, a group opposing the Sandinista government in Nicaragua. A seven-year investigation by an independent counsel found no direct evidence that the president knew of the diversion.

President Reagan at the Brandenburg Gate

1987

On a visit to Europe, President Reagan speaks at Berlin's Brandenburg Gate.

"General Secretary Gorbachev, if you seek peace, if you seek prosperity for the Soviet Union and Eastern Europe, if you seek liberalization: Come here to this gate! Mr. Gorbachev, open this gate! Mr. Gorbachev, tear down this wall!"

—PRESIDENT RONALD REAGAN, at the Brandenburg Gate

1987

After Secretary Gorbachev agrees not to link reduction of intermediate range missiles with SDI, he and President Reagan sign an agreement in Washington, D.C., to begin destroying this group of weapons. Each side will have on-site monitoring of the other.

"Dovorey no provorey."

—PRESIDENT RONALD REAGAN, repeating a Russian saying, "Trust, but verify"

1988

For his final summit with Secretary Gorbachev, President Reagan visits Moscow.

"Freedom . . . is the right to put forth an idea, scoffed at by the experts, and watch it catch fire among the people. It is the right to dream—to follow your dream or stick to your conscience, even if you're the only one in a sea of doubters."

—PRESIDENT RONALD REAGAN, speaking to students at Moscow State University

1988

Republican vice president George H. W. Bush defeats Massachusetts governor Michael Dukakis and becomes the first sitting vice president to be elected to the presidency since Martin Van Buren.

> "I *want a kinder, gentler nation*."
>
> —GEORGE H. W. BUSH, accepting the Republican nomination

1989

As the world watches, the Berlin Wall comes down.

THE FALL OF THE BERLIN WALL MARKED THE BEGINNING OF THE END OF THE DIVISION OF EUROPE. NATIONS THAT HAD BEEN DOMINATED BY THE SOVIET UNION BECAME INDEPENDENT SOVEREIGN STATES AND SOUGHT ALLIANCES WITH THE WEST. IN 1990, WITH BUSH ADMINISTRATION SUPPORT, GERMANY WAS REUNITED. IN 1991 THE SOVIET UNION CEASED TO EXIST.

1989

After a year in which Panamanian strongman Manuel Noriega threatened American lives in Panama, overrode election results in that country, and was himself indicted in Florida for drug trafficking, President Bush authorizes Operation Just Cause, and American troops invade Panama. Noriega will be brought to Miami for trial, and the way will be paved for democratic elections.

1990

President Bush signs the Americans with Disabilities Act into law. It prohibits employment discrimination against qualified individuals with disabilities.

1990

Saddam Hussein invades Kuwait. The United Nations Security Council imposes sanctions on Iraq, and the United States begins to build a coalition to reverse Iraqi aggression.

> *"This will not stand."*
>
> —PRESIDENT GEORGE H. W. BUSH

1990

As part of a budget compromise with the Democrat-controlled Congress, President Bush, who said there would be no new taxes in his administration, signs a deficit reduction bill that includes a tax hike.

1991

With both the United Nations Security Council and the U.S. Congress having approved the use of force, the United States begins Operation Desert Storm. An air campaign is followed by a ground war of one hundred hours.

PRESIDENT GEORGE H. W. BUSH IN PERSIAN GULF

"Kuwait is liberated. Iraq's army is defeated. Our military objectives are met."

—PRESIDENT GEORGE H. W. BUSH

SADDAM HUSSEIN WAS DEFEATED BUT STILL IN POWER. ON APRIL 3, 1991, THE UNITED NATIONS SECURITY COUNCIL ORDERED THE GOVERNMENT OF IRAQ TO DECLARE ITS WEAPONS OF MASS DESTRUCTION PROGRAMS, TO ACCEPT DESTRUCTION OF CHEMICAL AND BIOLOGICAL WEAPONS, AND TO SUBMIT TO AN INSPECTIONS REGIME. THE INTERNATIONAL ATOMIC ENERGY AGENCY WAS MANDATED TO VERIFY ELIMINATION OF IRAQ'S NUCLEAR WEAPONS PROGRAM.

1991

The DOS version of America Online is launched. AOL will bring millions not familiar with computers to the online world.

1992

When a jury in a California state court finds four policemen not guilty of excessive force in the arrest of Rodney King, riots break out in Los Angeles. The policemen, who have been seen on a videotape beating King, will be charged in federal court, and two of them will be found guilty of violating his civil rights.

1992

President George H. W. Bush, whose approval ratings neared 90 percent at the end of the Persian Gulf War, is defeated by Arkansas governor Bill Clinton. For the first time since the Carter administration, the Democrats will control the presidency and both houses of Congress.

"The economy, stupid."

—Advice posted in the Clinton campaign headquarters

THE ECONOMY, WIDELY BELIEVED TO BE FALTERING AT THE TIME OF THE 1992 ELECTION, WAS IN FACT DOING WELL. THE GROSS DOMESTIC PRODUCT GREW AT AN AVERAGE RATE OF ABOVE 4 PERCENT FOR THE YEAR AND WAS AT 4.5 PERCENT DURING THE LAST QUARTER OF THE YEAR, WHEN THE ELECTION WAS HELD.

1992

President Bush sends American troops to Somalia to provide security and stability so that international organizations can deliver food and medicine to hundreds of thousands of starving Somalis.

1993

The new president takes the oath of office.

"And so, my fellow Americans, at the edge of the twenty-first century, let us begin with energy and hope, with faith and discipline, and let us work until our work is done."

—President Bill Clinton

ONE OF THE NEW PRESIDENT'S FIRST ACTS WAS TO APPOINT HIS WIFE, HILLARY RODHAM CLINTON, TO HEAD A TASK FORCE ON HEALTH-CARE REFORM.

1993

Islamic fundamentalists drive a rental van armed with a bomb into the basement of New York's World Trade Center, where it explodes, killing six. Ramzi Yousef, who masterminded the bombing, and five others will be sentenced to life imprisonment.

Yousef's uncle, Khalid Sheikh Mohammed, masterminded the 2001 attack on the World Trade Center.

1993

President Clinton signs the Omnibus Budget Reconciliation Act, which contains a $240 billion tax increase.

1993

After the signing of the Oslo Peace Accords, Israeli prime minister Yitzhak Rabin and Palestine Liberation Organization (PLO) head Yasir Arafat shake hands on the White House lawn.

In the accords the PLO recognized the right of Israel to exist, which raised hopes for Middle East peace. Arafat dashed these hopes in 2000 when, despite major concessions by Ehud Barak, who was then prime minister of Israel, he refused to enter into any kind of agreement.

1993

President Clinton sends additional troops to Somalia as part of an effort to capture Somali warlord Mohammed Aidid.

1993

With presidents Gerald R. Ford, Jimmy Carter, and George H. W. Bush looking on, President Clinton signs the North American Free Trade Agreement (NAFTA), which lowers tariffs between the United States, Canada, and Mexico.

President Clinton signing NAFTA

1993

Two Black Hawk helicopters are downed and eighteen Americans are killed in Somalia. The United States shortly thereafter withdraws its forces.

1994

Mrs. Clinton's health-care plan, fiercely debated for the expanded role it foresees for government, dies without ever coming to a vote in Congress.

1995

The Republicans, who have campaigned on the Contract

with America, which promises to reduce the size and intrusiveness of government, take control of the House of Representatives. Newt Gingrich becomes the first Republican Speaker in forty years.

IN THE FIRST ONE HUNDRED DAYS OF THE NEW CONGRESS, NINE OF THE TEN ITEMS IN THE CONTRACT PASSED THE HOUSE, THOUGH NOT ALL MADE IT THROUGH THE SENATE OR PAST THE PRESIDENT'S VETO PEN. ONE PIECE OF LEGISLATION, THE LINE-ITEM VETO, WAS RULED UNCONSTITUTIONAL BY THE SUPREME COURT.

1995

A bomb inside a rental truck destroys the Alfred P. Murrah Federal Building in Oklahoma City, Oklahoma, killing 168, including 19 children. Timothy McVeigh will be sentenced to death and executed for the bombing; Terry Nichols, sentenced to life in prison.

> *"You have lost too much, but you have not lost everything. And you have certainly not lost America, for we will stand with you for as many tomorrows as it takes."*
>
> —President Bill Clinton, at the Oklahoma City memorial service, speaking to the families of those who were killed

1995

After three years of war in Bosnia, where Serbs are killing and displacing Bosnian Muslims, the president organizes peace talks in Dayton, Ohio. When agreement is reached, he sends American troops into Bosnia as part of a NATO peacekeeping force.

The Dayton Peace Accords addressed only some of the problems that arose as a result of the post–Cold War breakup of Yugoslavia. Even as the accords were signed, tensions were escalating between Serbs and Albanian Muslims in Kosovo.

1996

Mrs. Clinton is called to testify before a grand jury about Whitewater, a land venture in Arkansas that involved then governor Bill Clinton, Mrs. Clinton, and Mrs. Clinton's law firm. Accusations about Whitewater and other matters would swirl about the White House during most of the eight years President Clinton was in office.

1996

Terrorists explode a truck bomb outside Khobar Towers, a housing complex in Saudi Arabia, killing nineteen U.S. servicemen.

Other terrorist assaults on Americans abroad followed: 1998 truck bomb attacks on U.S. embassies in Kenya and Tanzania; and a 2000 bomb attack on the USS *Cole*, in port in Yemen, which killed seventeen American sailors.

1996

After vetoing two welfare reform bills passed by the Republican Congress, President Clinton signs a third one. It places a five-year limit on welfare benefits, encourages work, and will help millions of people move from dependency to self-sufficiency.

1996

President Clinton is reelected, becoming the first Democratic president since Franklin D. Roosevelt to be elected to a second term.

1998

The world learns that the president may have had an inappropriate relationship with a White House intern, Monica Lewinsky. He denies the charge but later in the year will admit to it.

> "It *depends on what the meaning of the word* is *is*."
> —PRESIDENT BILL CLINTON

1998

The House of Representatives votes two articles of impeachment against the president, one for perjury and one for obstructing justice. The charges relate to the Monica Lewinsky case and to the matter of Paula Jones, to whom the president has agreed to pay $850,000 to settle a sexual harassment suit.

ALTHOUGH PRESIDENT CLINTON'S PERSONAL APPROVAL RATINGS WITH THE PUBLIC WERE LOW IN THE IMPEACHMENT PERIOD AND BEYOND, HIS JOB APPROVAL NUMBERS REMAINED HIGH.

1999

In his State of the Union message, President Clinton notes record economic expansion and a federal budget that is balanced for the first time in thirty years.

A Democratic president and a Republican Congress achieved the balanced budget, their efforts greatly aided by the peace dividend: Since 1989, the year that the Berlin Wall came down, the percentage of the nation's gross domestic product going to defense had fallen 46 percent.

1999

President Clinton is acquitted of impeachment charges when only 45 senators vote to convict him on the charge of perjury and 55 vote against. On the obstruction charge the Senate splits evenly, 50–50. Sixty-seven votes are necessary to convict.

At the end of Clinton's presidency, the independent counsel agreed to drop further investigations into these matters. The president, saying he had testified falsely, agreed to a five-year suspension of his Arkansas law license and a $25,000 fine.

"*I have apologized for my conduct and I have done my best to atone for it with my family, my administration and the American people. I have paid a high price for it, which I accept because it caused so much pain to so many people.*"

—President Bill Clinton

1999

To help end Serb violence against Albanian Muslims in Kosovo, the United States takes part in a NATO bombing campaign. Serbian leader Slobodan Milosevic withdraws his troops from Kosovo.

1999

On the mall in Washington, D.C., ground is broken for the National Museum of the American Indian.

> *"I think the majority of people in America know it's time for the Indians to have a reemergence in this nation."*
>
> —U.S. senator BEN NIGHTHORSE CAMPBELL

CELEBRATING THE OPENING OF THE NATIONAL MUSEUM OF THE AMERICAN INDIAN

1999

As its thirty-fifth anniversary approaches, Moore's Law proves to be a remarkably accurate forecast.

IN 1965 GORDON E. MOORE, COFOUNDER OF INTEL, PREDICTED THAT THE NUMBER OF TRANSISTORS ON AN INTEGRATED CIRCUIT WOULD DOUBLE

EVERY YEAR, A PREDICTION HE REVISED IN 1975 TO SAY THEY WOULD DOUBLE EVERY TWO YEARS. IN THE TIME SINCE THEY HAVE DOUBLED ABOUT EVERY EIGHTEEN MONTHS, AND WITH THAT INCREASE COMPUTER POWER HAS GROWN EXPONENTIALLY AND COMPUTER COSTS HAVE DECLINED.

"There is certainly no end to creativity."
—Gordon E. Moore

As the century ended, work remained to open the opportunities of a free society to every citizen, but Americans of all races, male and female, were rising to the top of national life. At the Department of State, where the first secretary had been Thomas Jefferson, the top office was held by a woman. She would be succeeded by an African-American secretary of state, and he by an African-American woman.

Over the course of the twentieth century, the United States had first defeated Fascism, then triumphed over Communism. An American political scientist, Francis Fukuyama, made a provocative suggestion: that the great struggle of ideologies was over and that democracy had won.

"What we may be witnessing is not just the end of the cold war, or the passing of a particular period of postwar history, but the end of history as such: that is, the end point of mankind's ideological evolution and the universalization of Western liberal democracy as the final form of human government."

—Francis Fukuyama

OTHERS WERE NOT SO CERTAIN THAT THE END OF HISTORY HAD ARRIVED. THEY THOUGHT IT POSSIBLE THAT DEMOCRACY'S GREATEST CHALLENGES MIGHT LIE AHEAD.

SEVEN

THE CALLING OF OUR TIME

2000

According to the census the population of the United States is 281,421,906.

2000

The presidential election comes down to Florida, where Governor George W. Bush of Texas has a narrow lead. After the supreme court of Florida orders a statewide recount of "undervotes" (ballots on which machines failed to detect a vote for president), the U.S. Supreme Court accepts a petition to review the process. Seven of nine justices rule that the recount is unconstitutional because inconsistent and changing standards are being used to count the ballots. On the ground that a recount meeting constitutional standards is impossible before the December 12 statutory deadline for states choosing electors, five of nine justices rule that the recount must stop. Florida officials then certify that Governor Bush has won Florida's presidential electors.

ALTHOUGH VICE PRESIDENT AL GORE WON MORE POPULAR VOTES THAN GEORGE W. BUSH, THE TEXAS GOVERNOR WON IN THE ELECTORAL COLLEGE AND BECAME PRESIDENT OF THE UNITED STATES.

2001

George W. Bush is sworn in as president.

"After the Declaration of Independence was signed, Virginia statesman John Page wrote to Thomas Jefferson: '. . . Do you not think an angel rides in the whirlwind and directs this storm?'"

—President George W. Bush, in his inaugural address

2001

On September 11, nineteen militant Islamists armed with knives and box cutters hijack four commercial airliners. They fly two into the World Trade Center in New York and another into the Pentagon in Washington, D.C. A fourth plane goes down in a field in Pennsylvania as the passengers battle the hijackers for control of the aircraft. Almost three thousand are killed.

The raising of the flag at Ground Zero

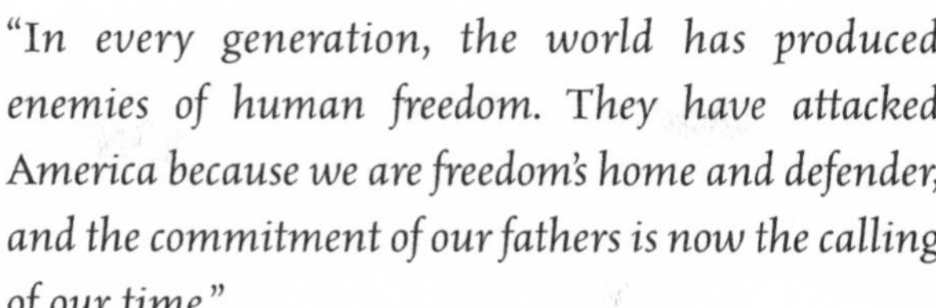

"In every generation, the world has produced enemies of human freedom. They have attacked America because we are freedom's home and defender, and the commitment of our fathers is now the calling of our time."

—PRESIDENT GEORGE W. BUSH

BIBLIOGRAPHY

Sources and Acknowledgments

The most important sources for constructing this time line were the firsthand accounts written by men and women like Puritan leader William Bradford, orator and activist Frederick Douglass, and southern diarist Mary Chesnut. Access to letters, diaries, and other original sources and documents is now easier than it has ever been. There are collections aimed at a variety of audiences, from the American Voices series for young readers published by Benchmark Books, to Noel Rae's *Witnessing America: The Library of Congress Book of Firsthand Accounts of Life in America, 1600–1900* (New York: Stonesong Press, 1996). There are also a growing number of Web sites where one can find original documents, including the National Archives (http://www.archives.gov), American Memory at the Library of Congress (http://memory.loc.gov/ammem), the American Presidency Project (http://www.presidency.ucsb.edu), American Journeys (http://www.americanjourneys.org), the Early Americas Digital Archive (http://www.mith2.umd.edu:8080/eada/index.jsp), the University of Virginia Library Electronic Text Center (http://etext.lib.virginia.edu), the National Museum of American History (http://americanhistory.si.edu), the Avalon Project (http://www.yale.edu/lawweb/avalon/avalon.htm), and FindLaw (http://www.findlaw.com).

That said, research is still a collaborative human enterprise, and many people in libraries, museums, and universities aided in the search for needed information. I'd especially like to thank Beth Davis-Brown, John Hebert, Ernest Emrich, Marvin Kranz, Janice Ruth, and Mary Yarnall at the Library of Congress; Maggie Dittemore and Dennis Stanford at the National Museum of

Natural History; Jeremy Bangs at the Leiden American Pilgrim Museum; Peter Drummey at the Massachusetts Historical Society; Tamara Elliott at the U.S. Senate Library; Michael Gannon at the University of Florida; Andrea B. Goldstein at the Harvard University Archives; Stephen Hardin of Victoria College; John L. Kessell of the University of New Mexico; Dona M. McDermott at Valley Forge National Historical Park; Regina Oliver at the U.S. Census Bureau Library; Donald Ritchie of the U.S. Senate Historical Office; P. S. Ruckman Jr. of Rock Valley College; Lesley Schoenfeld of the Harvard Law School Library; Juri Stratford at Shields Library at the University of California; Thad W. Tate of the College of William and Mary; Amy Verone at Sagamore Hill National Historic Site; Dennis J. Vetrovec at Indiana State University Library; and Erik Villard at the U.S. Army Center of Military History.

A number of reference works were useful as I constructed this time line, including *Africana: The Encyclopedia of the African and African American Experience*, edited by Kwame Anthony Appiah and Henry Louis Gates Jr. (New York: Basic *Civitas* Books, 1999); *Handbook of North American Indians*, a multivolume project edited by William C. Sturtevant (Washington, D.C.: Smithsonian Institution, 1978–); and *Notable American Women*, a project originally undertaken at Radcliffe College, now grown to five volumes (Cambridge, Mass.: Harvard University Press, Belknap Press, 1971–2004). In the course of working on this project, I was also happy to discover well-written and generally reliable textbooks such as *The American Nation: A History of the United States*, 10th ed., by John A. Garraty and Mark C. Carnes (New York: Longman, 2000); *America: A Narrative History*, 5th ed., by George Brown Tindall and David Emory Shi (New York: Norton, 1999); and *The Story of America: Freedom and Crisis from Settlement to Superpower*, by

Allen Weinstein and David Rubel (New York: Agincourt Press, 2002).

I also depended on secondary sources for guidance, and among the books and articles I found to be useful and enlightening are those that follow:

Ambrose, Stephen E. *Eisenhower: Soldier and President.* New York: Touchstone, 1991.

____. *Nothing Like It in the World: The Men Who Built the Transcontinental Railroad, 1863–1869.* New York: Touchstone, 2001.

____. *Undaunted Courage: Meriwether Lewis, Thomas Jefferson, and the Opening of the American West.* New York: Simon & Schuster, 1996.

American Heritage, ed. *Great Minds of History.* Interviews by Roger Mudd. New York: Wiley, 1999.

Avrich, Paul. *Sacco and Vanzetti: The Anarchist Background.* Princeton, N.J.: Princeton University Press, 1991.

Bailyn, Bernard. *The Peopling of British North America: An Introduction.* New York: Knopf, 1986.

Barry, John M. *The Great Influenza: The Epic Story of the Deadliest Plague in History.* New York: Penguin Books, 2005.

Battis, Emery. *Saints and Sectaries: Anne Hutchinson and the Antinomian Controversy in the Massachusetts Bay Colony.* Chapel Hill: University of North Carolina Press, 1962.

Beschloss, Michael R. *The Crisis Years: Kennedy and Khrushchev, 1960–1963.* New York: Edward Burlingame Books, 1991.

Billings, Warren M. *A Little Parliament: The Virginia General Assembly in the Seventeenth Century.* Richmond: Library of Virginia, in partnership with Jamestown 2007 / Jamestown-Yorktown Foundation, 2004.

Boot, Max. *The Savage Wars of Peace: Small Wars and the Rise of American Power.* New York: Basic Books, 2002.

Brookhiser, Richard. *Alexander Hamilton, American.* New York: Touchstone, 2000.

Brooks, Victor. *The Boston Campaign: April 1775–March 1776.* Conshohocken, Pa.: Combined Publishing, 1999.

Bush, George, and Brent Scowcroft. *A World Transformed.* New York: Knopf, 1998.

Cannon, Lou. *President Reagan: The Role of a Lifetime.* New York: PublicAffairs, 2000.

———. *Ronald Reagan: The Presidential Portfolio; A History Illustrated from the Collection of the Ronald Reagan Library and Museum.* New York: PublicAffairs, 2001.

Chernow, Ron. *Alexander Hamilton.* New York: Penguin, 2004.

———. *Titan: The Life of John D. Rockefeller, Sr.* New York: Vintage Books, 1999.

Coffey, Michael, ed. *The Irish in America.* With text by Terry Golway. New York: Hyperion, 1997.

Colman, Penny. *A Woman Unafraid: The Achievements of Frances Perkins.* New York: Atheneum, 1993.

Daniels, John D. "The Indian Population of North America in 1492." *William and Mary Quarterly,* 3rd ser., 49, no. 2 (April 1992): 298–320.

DeVoto, Bernard. *The Year of Decision: 1846.* New York: Truman Talley Books, 2000.

Ellis, Joseph J. *American Sphinx: The Character of Thomas Jefferson.* New York: Vintage Books, 1998.

———. *His Excellency: George Washington.* New York: Knopf, 2004.

Evans, Harold. *The American Century.* New York: Knopf, 1998.

———. *They Made America: From the Steam Engine to the Search Engine; Two Centuries of Innovators.* New York: Little, Brown, 2004.

Fehrenbach, T. R. *This Kind of War: The Classic Korean War History.* 50th anniv. ed. Washington, D.C.: Brassey's, 2000.

Fischer, David Hackett. *Albion's Seed: Four British Folkways in America.* New York: Oxford University Press, 1991.

____. *Paul Revere's Ride.* New York: Oxford University Press, 1994.

____. *Washington's Crossing.* New York: Oxford University Press, 2004.

Flexner, Eleanor, and Ellen Fitzpatrick. *Century of Struggle: The Woman's Rights Movement in the United States.* Enl. ed. Cambridge, Mass.: Harvard University Press, Belknap Press, 1996.

Foner, Eric. *Reconstruction: America's Unfinished Revolution, 1863–1877.* New York: Perennial Classics, 2002.

Ford, Henry Jones. *The Scotch-Irish in America.* New York: Peter Smith, 1941.

Fukuyama, Francis. "The End of History?" *National Interest*, no. 16 (Summer 1989): 3–18.

Gordon, John Steele. *An Empire of Wealth: The Epic History of American Economic Power.* New York: HarperCollins, 2004.

Gragg, Larry. "Order vs. Liberty." *American History*, October 1998. http://www.thehistorynet.com/ah/blorderverusliberty/.

Greenhaw, Wayne. *Montgomery: The River City.* Montgomery, Ala.: River City Publishing, 2002.

Griffith, Elisabeth. *In Her Own Right: The Life of Elizabeth Cady Stanton.* New York: Oxford University Press, 1985.

Hadingham, Evan. "America's First Immigrants." *Smithsonian*, November 1, 2004: 90–94.

Halberstam, David. *The Fifties.* New York: Fawcett Books, 1994.

Horton, James Oliver, and Lois E. Horton. *Slavery and the Making of America.* New York: Oxford University Press, 2005.

Johnson, Paul. *A History of the American People.* New York: HarperPerennial, 1999.

Karnow, Stanley. *Vietnam: A History*. Rev. ed. New York: Penguin Books, 1991.

Keegan, John. *The First World War*. New York: Vintage Books, 2000.

____. *The Second World War*. New York: Viking, 1990.

Kennedy, David M. *Freedom from Fear: The American People in Depression and War, 1929–1945*. New York: Oxford University Press, 2001.

Kissinger, Henry. *White House Years*. Boston: Little, Brown, 1979.

____. *Years of Renewal*. New York: Simon & Schuster, 1999.

____. *Years of Upheaval*. Boston: Little, Brown, 1982.

Klein, Maury. *Rainbow's End: The Crash of 1929*. New York: Oxford University Press, 2003.

Larson, Erik. *The Devil in the White City: Murder, Magic, and Madness at the Fair That Changed America*. New York: Vintage Books, 2004.

Larson, T. A. *History of Wyoming*. 2nd ed. Lincoln: University of Nebraska Press, 1978.

MacNeil, Neil. *Forge of Democracy: The House of Representatives*. New York: David McKay, 1963.

Manchester, William. *American Caesar: Douglas MacArthur, 1880–1964*. Boston: Little, Brown, 1978.

McCullough, David. *John Adams*. New York: Touchstone, 2002.

____. *Truman*. New York: Touchstone, 1993.

McDougall, Walter A. *Freedom Just Around the Corner: A New American History, 1585–1828*. New York: HarperCollins, 2004.

McPherson, James M. *The Illustrated Battle Cry of Freedom: The Civil War Era*. New York: Oxford University Press, 2003.

Morison, Samuel Eliot. *The Great Explorers: The European Discovery of America*. New York: Oxford University Press, 1978.

____. *The Two-Ocean War: A Short History of the United States Navy in the Second World War*. Boston: Back Bay Books, 1989.

Morison, Samuel Eliot, and Henry Steele Commager. *The Growth of the American Republic*. 4th ed. 2 vols. New York: Oxford University Press, 1950.

Morris, Edmund. *The Rise of Theodore Roosevelt*. New York: Ballantine Books, 1980.

Murphy, Jim. *An American Plague: The True and Terrifying Story of the Yellow Fever Epidemic of 1793*. New York: Clarion Books, 2003.

Murrow, Edward R., and Fred W. Friendly, eds. *See It Now*. New York: Simon & Schuster, 1955.

Neillands, Robin. *The Bomber War: The Allied Air Offensive Against Nazi Germany*. Woodstock, N.Y.: Overlook Press, 2001.

O'Toole, Patricia. *When Trumpets Call: Theodore Roosevelt After the White House*. New York: Simon & Schuster, 2005.

Patterson, James T. *Grand Expectations: The United States, 1945–1974*. New York: Oxford University Press, 1997.

Peterson, Merrill D. *The Great Triumvirate: Webster, Clay, and Calhoun*. New York: Oxford University Press, 1987.

Remini, Robert V. *The Life of Andrew Jackson*. New York: Harper & Row, 1988.

Schlesinger, Arthur M., Jr. *The Age of Roosevelt*. 3 vols. Boston: Houghton Mifflin, 1957–60.

Shattan, Joseph. *Architects of Victory: Six Heroes of the Cold War*. Washington, D.C.: Heritage Foundation, 1999.

Smith, Carl. *Urban Disorder and the Shape of Belief: The Great Chicago Fire, the Haymarket Bomb, and the Model Town of Pullman*. Chicago: University of Chicago Press, 1995.

Starrs, James E. "Once More Unto the Breech: The Firearms Evidence in the Sacco and Vanzetti Case Revisited." Pts. 1 and 2. *Journal of Forensic Sciences* 31, no. 2 (April 1986): 630–54; no. 3 (July 1986): 1050–78.

Stegner, Wallace. *The Gathering of Zion: The Story of the Mormon Trail*. Lincoln: University of Nebraska Press, 1992.

Sulzberger, C. L., and the eds. of *American Heritage*. *The American Heritage Picture History of World War II*. Edited by David McCullough. New York: American Heritage Publishing, 1966.

Thornton, Russell. "Trends Among American Indians in the United States." In *America Becoming: Racial Trends and Their Consequences*, vol. 1, edited by Neil J. Smelser, William Julius Wilson, and Faith Mitchell, 135–69. Washington, D.C.: National Academy Press, 2001. http://www.nap.edu/books/030906838X/html/135.html.

Thurston, Robert H. *Robert Fulton: His Life and Its Results*. New York: Dodd, Mead, 1891. http://www.history.rochester.edu/steam/thurston/fulton/.

Ubelaker, Douglas H. "North American Indian Population Size, A.D. 1500 to 1985." *American Journal of Physical Anthropology* 77 (1988): 289–94.

Von Drehle, David. *Triangle: The Fire That Changed America*. New York: Grove Press, 2003.

Ward, Geoffrey C. *The Civil War: An Illustrated History*. New York: Knopf, 1990.

———. *The West: An Illustrated History*. Boston: Little, Brown, 1996.

Weinstein, Allen, and Alexander Vassiliev. *The Haunted Wood: Soviet Espionage in America—the Stalin Era*. New York: Modern Library, 2000.

Williams, Juan. *Eyes on the Prize: America's Civil Rights Years, 1954–1965*. New York: Penguin, 1988.

Willison, George F. *Saints and Strangers*. New ed. New York: Ballantine Books, 1965.

Wirt, William. *Sketches of the Life and Character of Patrick Henry.* Philadelphia: James Webster, 1817. Reprint, Chapel Hill: University of North Carolina at Chapel Hill, 1999, available at http://docsouth.unc.edu/wirt/wirt.html.

Wood, Gordon S. *The Radicalism of the American Revolution.* New York: Knopf, 1992.

ILLUSTRATION CREDITS

Section One

p. 1: Engraving of *Mayflower* based on a painting by Marshall Johnson (1850–1921), Bettmann/CORBIS; p. 4: George H. H. Huey/CORBIS; p. 5: Undated woodcut, Bettmann/CORBIS; p. 10: Painting based on an engraving made from life, Bettmann/CORBIS; p. 11: Nineteenth-century painting by John Leon Gerome Ferris, Bettmann/CORBIS; p. 13: Contemporary illustration by Joost Hartgers, Museum of the City of New York, CORBIS; p. 19: Nineteenth-century engraving based on a painting by Benjamin West, Bettmann/CORBIS; p. 22: Engraving based on a 1767 painting made from life by David Martin, The Granger Collection, NY.

Section Two

p. 25: Washington taking command of the Continental Army, 1875 wood engraving, The Granger Collection, NY; p. 31: Currier & Ives lithograph, Bettmann/CORBIS; p. 32: Pastels from life by Benjamin Blyth, The Granger Collection, NY; p. 35: Late-eighteenth-century English engraving, The Granger Collection, NY; p. 37: Steel engraving based on a painting by John Trumbull, in which many portraits were done from life, The Granger Collection, NY; p. 39: 1851 painting by Emanuel Leutze, The Granger Collection, NY; p. 42: Unknown artist, The Library of Congress; p. 45: Nineteenth-century engraving, The Granger Collection, NY; p. 46: 1802 painting by John Trumbull, The Granger Collection, NY; p. 48: 1790 engraving by Amos Doolittle, The Granger Collection, NY; p. 52: Contemporary painting, The Granger Collection, NY; p. 55: Contemporary watercolor by William Birch, The Granger Collection, NY.

Section Three

p. 57: *Storming Fort Wagner*, a circa 1890 lithograph portraying the 54th Massachusetts Regiment in 1863, The Library of Congress; p. 61: Painting by Thomas Mickell Burnham (1818–1866), Private Collection/Bridgeman Art Gallery; p. 62: 1842 wood engraving, The Granger Collection, NY; p. 65: Engraving by William Strickland based on a circa 1815 work by George Munger, The Granger Collection, NY; p. 66: Circa 1856 lithograph by Charles Severin, The Library of Congress; p. 73: Royalty-Free/CORBIS; p. 74: 1854 steel engraving, The Granger Collection, NY; p. 77: Undated engraving, Bettmann/CORBIS; p. 79: 1869 oil painting by Albert Bierstadt, Butler Institute of American Art, Youngstown, OH, USA, Gift of Joseph G. Butler III, 1946, Bridgeman Art Library; p. 84: Circa 1855 engraving by Robert Whitechurch based on a drawing by P. F. Rothermel, The Library of Congress; p. 85: Engraving based on a 1853 drawing by George Richmond, The Granger Collection, NY; p. 88: Undated engraving based on photographs, Bettmann/CORBIS; p. 90: June 3, 1860, photograph, The Granger Collection, NY; p. 95 (left): Circa 1866 chromolithograph, The Library of Congress; p. 95 (right): 1863 photograph, Julian Vannerson, The Library of Congress; p. 95 (bottom): Nineteenth-century lithograph, The Library of Congress; p. 97: February 9, 1864, photograph by Anthony Berger for the Brady Studio, The Library of Congress; p. 100: 1865 photograph by Alexander Gardner, The Granger Collection, NY.

Section Four

p. 101: Meeting of railroads at Promontory Summit, Union Pacific RR, Bettmann/CORBIS; p. 107: Contemporary lithograph, Bettmann/CORBIS; p. 108: Circa 1881 photograph by Napoleon Sarony, Bettmann/CORBIS; p. 109: Union Pacific Museum;

p. 111: The Library of Congress; p. 112: 1873 lithograph by Thomas Moran, author's collection; p. 114: Bettmann/CORBIS; p. 116: CORBIS; p. 117: Bettmann/CORBIS; p. 118 (left): Circa 1899 photograph, The Granger Collection, NY; p. 118 (right): Circa 1918 photograph, The Granger Collection, NY; p. 119: 1884 cartoon, The Granger Collection, NY; p. 122: Circa 1885 Currier & Ives chromolithograph, The Library of Congress; p. 125: Circa 1900 photograph, The Granger Collection, NY; p. 127: Frances Benjamin Johnston, The Library of Congress; p. 129: Circa 1896 photograph, The Library of Congress; p. 131: William Dinwiddie, The Library of Congress; p. 133: Engraving, The Library of Congress; p. 136: John T. Daniels, NASA; p. 138: Bettmann/CORBIS.

Section Five

p. 145: Iwo Jima flag raising by Joe Rosenthal, AP/Wide World Photos; p. 148: Bettmann/CORBIS; p. 152: The Library of Congress; p. 153: Howard Chandler Christy, Swim Ink 2, LLC/CORBIS; p. 158: CORBIS; p. 159: Bettmann/CORBIS; p. 163: The Library of Congress; p. 165: AP/Wide World Photos; p. 167: AP/Wide World Photos; p. 168: Lewis Hine, National Archives; p. 170: 1938 photograph by Dorothea Lange, The Library of Congress; p. 173: AP/Wide World Photos; p. 175: AP/Wide World Photos; p. 177: AP/Wide World Photos; p. 178: National Archives; p. 182: AP/Wide World Photos; p. 184: The Granger Collection, NY; p. 185: AP/Wide World Photos; p. 188: National Archives.

Section Six

p. 189: Getty Images; p. 194: MLB Photos via Getty Images; p. 196: Bettmann/CORBIS; p. 198: Frank Cancellare, Bettmann/CORBIS; p. 202: Bettmann/CORBIS; p. 204: Bettmann/CORBIS; p. 205:

Bettmann/CORBIS; p. 206: Cass Gilbert, Bettmann/CORBIS; p. 208: Bettmann/CORBIS; p. 211: CORBIS; p. 215: AP/Wide World Photos; p. 216: Hulton-Deutsch Collection/CORBIS; p. 218: Bettmann/CORBIS; p. 222: Dirck Halstead, Bettmann/CORBIS; p. 223: Arthur Schatz/Time Life Pictures/Getty Images; p. 227: Time Life Pictures/NASA/Getty Images; p. 229: Dirck Halstead, Bettmann/CORBIS; p. 235: Bettmann/CORBIS; p. 238: CORBIS; p. 240: Bettmann/CORBIS; p. 241: Galen Rowell/CORBIS; p. 247: Wally McNamee/CORBIS; p. 250: Diana Walker/Time Life Pictures/Getty Images; p. 254: Ron Edmonds, AP/Wide World Photos; p. 259 (left): MOLLY RILEY/Reuters/CORBIS; p. 259 (center): JASON REED/Reuters/CORBIS; p. 259 (right): JASON REED/Reuters/CORBIS.

Section Seven

p. 263: Adam Woolfitt/CORBIS; p. 266: © 2001 (Bergen County, NJ) Thomas E. Franklin. Used by permission; p. 267: Alan Schein/zefa/CORBIS.

INDEX

Boldface numbers indicate pages with illustrations.

Index

Index

INDEX

Index

INDEX

INDEX

INDEX

INDEX

Index